living the adventure

Unmasking some sensitive problems through the lives and writings of Keith Miller and Bruce Larson

living the adventure

FAITH AND "HIDDEN" DIFFICULTIES

keith miller & bruce larson

word books, publisher
WACO TEXAS

First Printing—October, 1975
Second Printing—April, 1976
Third Printing—November, 1976
Fourth Printing—June, 1977
Fifth Printing—April, 1978
Sixth Printing—June, 1979
Seventh Printing—June, 1980
Eighth Printing—November, 1981
Ninth Printing—July, 1982
Tenth Printing—December, 1983
Eleventh Printing—October, 1984

LIVING THE ADVENTURE: FAITH AND "HIDDEN" DIFFICULTIES
by Keith Miller and Bruce Larson

ISBN 0-87680-892-5

Copyright © 1975 by Word Incorporated, Waco, Texas 76703. All rights reserved. No part of this book may be reproduced in any form, except for brief quotations in reviews, without the written permission of the publisher.

Library of Congress catalog card number: 75-27378
Printed in the United States of America

Unless otherwise noted, all Scripture quotations are from *The New English Bible,* © The Delegates of The Oxford University Press and The Syndics of The Cambridge University Press, 1961, 1970, and are used by permission.

Quotations marked RSV are from the Revised Standard Version of the Bible, copyrighted 1946 (renewed 1973), 1956 and © 1971 by the Division of Christian Education of the National Council of the Churches of Christ in the U.S.A., and are used by permission.

Contents

Acknowledgments	6
Introduction	7
1. Loneliness and Rejection	11
2. The Inner Life	27
3. Neighbor-Loving through Dialogue and Listening	45
4. Confession	63
5. Communicating "The Faith"	85
6. Money and Possessions	111
7. Power	129
8. Christian Sexuality	145
9. Christian Community and Uniqueness	167
10. Christian "Success"	185
11. Change, Risk and Growth	205
12. Sickness and Death	223
Notes	245
Sources	249

Acknowledgments

Although our names are the only two on the cover, this book is in many ways a team project. Our wives, Mary Allen and Hazel, not only went through the usual writer's wife's agony but did a great deal of hard work in editing and giving us critical help with the content—new and old—as it relates to our overall purpose.

The editors at Word and at Creative Resources went far beyond the help writers can expect from an editor. They sweated with us regarding the ideas and approach to education which this book (and course of the same name) represents.

We are also grateful to Joan Palmer who typed and retyped parts of the manuscript in quick time as our deadline approached.

The publishers and authors of the works cited have been most gracious in granting us permission to use the quotations included here.

We are only too aware that it is not possible to thank all of the people who helped in the conception and birth of a book like this. But you will notice that both of us have quoted frequently from the works of Dr. Paul Tournier. He has had a great influence in both our lives and has been a good friend and inspiration to us as we have tried to live the Adventure.

Keith Miller
Bruce Larson

Introduction

This book is written to those of you who have made a beginning commitment to God, but have run into hidden difficulties and hard questions you had not counted on.

We, Bruce Larson and Keith Miller, understand Christianity to be set realistically in the context of history and life. So we will deal more with problems as we actually experience them in relationships, rather than with doctrinal abstractions about how difficulties *should be* experienced and overcome ideally. As a matter of fact, both of us are continually uncovering new problems and still living with old unsolved ones, regardless of our best intentions. Also, neither of us claims to have "answers." But we believe there is value in expressing and trying to come to grips with the problems. We will deal with the issues which have been real in our experience as if we were sitting with you in your home.

As we got to know each other we found that regardless of the differences in our backgrounds and initial attempts at a serious personal commitment to God, there followed for both of us a strange awareness that we had entered a whole new segment of our lives. It was as if we had turned a page and begun a new chapter of life. We began to understand what Jesus meant when he said this fresh vision is like being "born again" (John 3:3, KJV). But as recently converted Christians, we discovered a whole new cluster of motivating needs and difficulties. We wanted to become different from what we had been. And this meant in practical terms that we were highly motivated to learn a whole new style of living. We felt that we were being freed from some of the limitations and fears we had always known. Our horizons began to expand, and we saw fresh possibilities of what we might become as loving persons. Our old dominant values changed. For one thing the frantic sense of responsibility for succeeding didn't seem as important when compared to learning about God and his will in ordinary life.

It is difficult to talk about such a change, but for both of us there was a profound sense of *relief*. The world *did* have meaning after all and so could our lives. And whether this reaction of relief was expressed in booming laughter, silent tears, or the pain of new insight, the *inner feeling* was one of joy and gratitude.

One of the most serious and unexpected problems we ran into almost immediately was that so many of our preconceptions about what it means to be a Christian were wrong. We didn't know what actually went on in the inner life of a converted person —except we assumed he must pray a good bit of the time.* We didn't really know how to love people or "hear" them. We certainly did not understand about the need for continuing confession or how to communicate the faith realistically without manipulating people. And we were both surprised when we experienced loneliness as "committed Christians."

When we tried to find out how a Christian wrestles with himself while dealing with these issues and things like money, power, sex, and sickness, we got mostly silence or "sermons" pointing to idealistic goals. But we discovered very little about the *painful process* of making decisions in these highly charged areas of life. It seems that in the Christian community there were various "official answers" to the gutsy problems of living. Then, too, there were hidden, underground solutions and directions each Christian had to hammer out on his own in order to survive in the world. Since no one we knew talked about the "hidden" level—where the real action took place for us—we felt almost ashamed to raise questions regarding the difficulties of trying to live in the real world as Christians. But we felt impelled to ask these hidden questions.

We filled in our ignorance with the stereotypes which buzz around any church like infectious mosquitoes. For example, as a child one of us thought of God as a strict judge and policeman, while the other saw him as a superkind old man who would never really lower the boom on anyone. Also we both assumed that Christians just sort of automatically know what prayer is—how to pray and how to put that knowledge to work. And many of the people we asked assumed the same things. But these preconceived

---

*We are very conscious of the many injustices done to women over the years and think it presumptuous that many male writers have referred to all persons as "he." In order to avoid the awkwardness and stylistic difficulties in always using both masculine and feminine pronouns, we will often use "he" in the traditional way. But we will mean *both* men and women unless it is obvious by the context that we mean only men.

notions did not square with our new experience. We were happy but sometimes scared and uncertain about what we ought to be thinking and doing.

It had not mattered how unreal our perceptions were concerning Christianity as long as we were merely attending church out of habit or training. The difficulties arose when we decided to commit as much of our lives as we honestly could to as much of God as we were able to understand at a given time. And when we made a specific commitment to try to live our whole lives for God, then it became very important to know things like: "What would God have me do in my situation—how can I find his will for me?" "Does he forgive people for the kinds of sins I've committed—even those I've never told anyone?" "How do I face the basic problem of loneliness and rejection as a Christian?" "How do I reconcile my need for power and success with the need to love others and serve God?"

In this book we are assuming that you have already made a beginning with God—that you want to live more lovingly and creatively in relationship to him, to other people, and to the person you might potentially become. It is out of this desire in our own lives that we are writing. Some of the material has appeared earlier in books or articles by each of us, but all of it relates to our own struggles to live for and learn about God as he is revealed in Jesus Christ.

Besides being written to the general audience, this is a reading book for a thirteen-week course for groups or classes called *Living the Adventure*. There are three cassettes, a study guide, and a leader's manual (besides this book), all produced by Creative Resources, P.O. Box 1790, Waco, Texas 76703. This course and book are sequels to *The Edge of Adventure*.

We want to warn you that this adventure may take you into experiences which could affect your whole life—and in directions neither you nor we can predict. As Alfred North Whitehead once pointed out about Columbus: Before he set sail he was dreaming of the Far East and of going around the world on a trackless ocean. But his dream failed and he never made it to China on his adventure. He did, however, discover America.

So if you have decided to come along with us, Welcome!

Bruce Larson
Keith Miller

Chapter One

Loneliness and Rejection

MEMORANDUM

TO: Keith
FROM: Bruce
RE: Chapter One—Loneliness and Rejection

Dear Keith:
    With all of the talk about the need for community today the fact remains that each of us in a particular sense begins and ends the Christian adventure alone.
    And since so many people—Christians and non-Christians—talk to me privately about being lonely, I think a good "hidden" problem to start this book with might be loneliness and feelings of rejection.
    Last winter I remember your telling me over the phone one afternoon that you had just experienced one of the loneliest times you could remember, but that out of it you had done a lot of thinking about what loneliness might mean.
    How about describing your feelings and thoughts that day and adding anything more you've found helpful?
                                                   Bruce

Last winter, I was sitting in a house at the beach, looking out the window and watching the driven gray rain blow the sea grass almost flat on the dunes. Alone in the house, I heard the wind howling, announcing the storm which was moving in from the Gulf. Ordinarily I would have felt an exciting surge of creativity and been inspired. But I was numb and simply stared blankly. I wasn't really numb. I could feel. My whole body ached and I had a sudden need to cry, to sob, but the tears would not come—too much training "to be a man."

At first I didn't know what was the matter. I knew I hadn't been able to write anything for months and felt that maybe I was through as a writer. I had driven myself so compulsively and for so long as a speaker and conference leader that speaking and leading conferences had lost their meaning for me. I felt like a "religious program" instead of an ordinary person. Although I still believed in God intellectually, I had pushed him away, and my prayers were sporadic and not very real. Something had gone very wrong. And as I looked at the future I couldn't see any meaning or purpose. I thought, "I guess I've done my thing." I felt very sad and old and something else much deeper.

Then I recognized where I was: in the desert of loneliness. There were certainly people who could have understood, but I could not bring myself to go to them somehow. This loneliness was not for companionship in the usual sense. It was a deeper thing. It was an experiencing of the fact that we are all really alone in the universe except for God—and for some reason I'd pushed him away. I wanted—I didn't even *know* what I wanted. But I was so miserable that I hurt physically, and I felt like a misfit and that no one really wanted me around except for what I could do in terms of performance. I felt like no one wanted just me—and that they would surely get tired of me if they had to be with me very long. It was that paranoid feeling one sometimes gets at a party or meeting when he senses that people might wish he hadn't come. What had started out to be loneliness had blossomed into self-pity.

I thought of other Christians I knew. But they all seemed to have many friends and to be untroubled by this loneliness. As I sat there I remembered a man I'd talked to several years ago. Jack was a very sharp and winsome person with a good sense of humor. He was a Christian minister, a district superintendent, whose position in his denomination makes him a pastor to fifty or sixty other ministers. He was handsome, intelligent, articulate, honest about himself, personally committed to Christ—and miserable.

As we talked, Jack told me that he felt basically lonely inside, even though he has a fine family and has done well in his vocation. He said that when he looked around at the other participants at ministers' meetings like the one we were attending, he felt as if many of his associates represented a kind of ingroup and had close personal friends with whom they came and roomed, but he was not able to be as personal with other people as they seemed to be. In fact he felt that he had very few truly close personal friends at all, and that made him feel inadequate and lonely—even though he ministers to people constantly and is surrounded by "Christian friends."

As we talked, I thought of my own life inside and how often over the years I have felt like a loner. I recalled as a youngster moving to a new city and looking at groups of boys who seemed to be close buddies and wishing I could be a real part of that which they seemed to be sharing. But then I became a part of such groups, and later fraternities, and was a leader in several. I was surprised to learn that, except in rare instances, ingroup members are not nearly as loving and vulnerable to each other about their real problems and aspirations as they appeared to be *from the outside*. I discovered the "façade of intimacy" which ingroups often wear. Some groups, including many churches, are apparently together so much because their individual members' identity is wrapped up in their association with the group, rather than because of any deep personal relationships with its members. But this façade of intimacy is a well-guarded secret, a secret which makes probably millions of kids and adults feel inadequate if they do not have "lots of close friends who are 'in'."

I am an outgoing person and have always moved toward people. Yet inwardly I am shy and reticent about imposing myself on those with whom I would most like to be friends. These past few years I have counseled with men and women, many of whom are successful materially and socially. I have found myself identifying so often with their feelings of inadequacy in this area of life that I began asking some of them how many really close personal friends they had. Many replied, "None." Some said, "One or two," but almost no one had more than five or six. After having moved more than fifteen times in twenty-five years of marriage, I realize that although there are many people we love, respond to, and enjoy being with on occasion, there are only a handful of people we feel are close friends.

All this made me wonder if perhaps many of us have been subtly conditioned to look for something which actually does not exist, except in a few cases—a successful place in life with a large number of intimate, totally open friends who could take away our most profound loneliness.

Existential Loneliness Universal

I realized as I sat at my window looking out on the beach, that the deepest kind of loneliness is universal and hits us again and again at each stage of life. I saw that no success, no loving wife or husband or intimate embrace or tender kiss, no community, no man or woman or child will ever be able to satisfy our desire to be released from our lonely condition. But this truth is so painful that we have repressed it, and some people will not allow themselves to experience their existential loneliness. Instead we fantasize the perfect marriage or ideal church rather than face the truth of our existence. So we keep hoping that one day we will find the friends who will really understand, the woman, or the man, who will bring peace to our restless life, the job in which we can fulfill our potential, the book which will explain it all, and the place where we can really feel at home.

But this refusal to accept the reality and basic givenness of our human loneliness leads us to make exhaustive demands on ourselves and the people around us. And finally we may become bitter and hostile when we start discovering that nobody and nothing can live up to our total expectations to save us from loneliness.

Reactions to Loneliness

Our reactions or responses largely determine whether loneliness can work as a creative, though painful, time, or build into a destructive neurotic episode of crossness and paranoid feelings of self-pity. I think it should be clear that there are different kinds of loneliness. The social kind can often be solved by getting off your chair and going to see people who may be lonely or whom you have neglected. Many times what we call loneliness is just self-centered passiveness. But there is also the irrational fear that people experience in loneliness. Some of this may be neurotic, and counseling could help. But some of it seems to go with the depersonalization and alienation almost built into modern life with the breakdown of social conventions and socializing institutions. But here I'm talking about the pervasive realization that we are alone in the world.

Panic and Run. When this pervasive loneliness comes, my temptation is to panic and run off in all directions trying frantically to "relate." Some people take on Christian committee assignments. Others grab a bottle, others a woman (or man). As we feel more frightened, we may fantasize growing old all alone with no one to really care. And we feel a sense of rising panic as we run after people socially or cling possessively to our children or friends. But our franticness at such times indicates that our interest is in ourselves and not in those we are trying to relate to, and our chances of true intimacy are not great.

Depression. Another temptation when loneliness "drops on us" is to get morbidly introspective and let our imaginations replay all of the selfish, thoughtless things people have done to us, or that we have done to them to "cause" our misery. This can lead to spiraling feelings of bitterness on the one hand or feelings of no worth on the other. And when the anger is turned in on ourselves we often get depressed.

Some Alternatives to Futility

But if we don't succumb to the temptation either to panic or to go into a depression, how can we handle the paralyzing storm clouds which come with the awareness of the loneliness of existence?

Begin with Prayer. Having tried both panic and depression I finally started the practice of getting up in the morning and asking God what he would say to me today "in this mess." And after a few minutes I usually have at least several specific things I need to do (sometimes just "get up and go to work"). But in any case by forcing myself to get up and get started after praying, I often avoid the days of introspection which seldom lead to anything but depressed feelings.

A Creative Way to Bury Your Head. Baron von Hügel related an analogy which has helped me to deal much more creatively with those periods of lonely desolation which occasionally sweep over my life. "I am traveling on a camel across a huge desert," he wrote. "Windless days occur and then all is well. But hurricanes of wind will come, unforeseen, tremendous. What to do then? It is very simple, but it takes much practice to do well at all. Dismount from the camel, fall prostrate face downwards on the sand, covering your head with your cloak. And lie thus, an hour, three hours, half a day; the sand storm will go, and you will arise, and continue your journey as if nothing had happened." [1] But von Hügel goes on to say that in such periods of lonely desolation there is a general rule of thumb: a person should form no conclusions, make no big decisions, nor change his course during such crises. And he particularly stresses not trying to force any particular religious mood on one's self. He advises us to turn gently to other things, to maintain a vague general attitude of acceptance or resignation, and to be gentle with ourselves and others. "The crisis," he says, "goes by, thus, with great fruit." [2]

This not panicking but doing little ordinary things when I am tempted to be paralyzed by either loneliness or emotional overload has proved very helpful to me. I catch up on my mail, write people I haven't written for a long time, file note cards, read articles or books I'm behind on and perhaps mow or trim the yard. One of our daughters washes her hair, does her laundry, gets her clothes in shape and cleans up her room. Since one *can* succeed at such little things and since they are not directly related to acceptance or rejection by other people, it is amazing how much more quickly this procedure helps the distinctive kind of panic or overly introspective loneliness to go away. And because I have in some sense been putting my house in order, I feel ready to begin again after such times of creative loneliness—to which one is tempted to react with fear, self-pity and frustration.

The Source of Loneliness

It seems to me increasingly that what is underneath all the layers of causes we attribute to loneliness is *fear*—the basic fear that goes along with being human and mortal. We fear that our lives will have no meaning, no purpose, that we will not be properly loved, that we will always be frustrated or that we will never find the ultimate acceptance we long for. And beneath it all —and all of these fears are often repressed—we fear to die, which we must do alone, without having really drunk the cup of life.

Help from Small Groups

One of the great functions of Christian small groups for me has been to provide a place where I can share feelings like these and discover that I am "not alone in my loneliness." And taking personal risks on the adventure to be vulnerable for God and people (with a group to come back to) somehow has helped me to overcome my basic human fears. For people have proved since the beginning of time that these fears cannot be gotten rid of by direct personal effort. Poets, military leaders, and psychologists have agreed that only a cause greater than our own interests can rid us of fear.* And the cause of living with Jesus Christ on his adventure to try to love the world and free it from fear—this commitment of our lives to Christ and his people is the only way I know to let loneliness drive me repeatedly back to God.

My experience has been that it is only God who answers the fears which lie beneath our most desperate loneliness.

God's Use of Loneliness and Rejection

What I am trying to say is that I believe existential loneliness and feelings of isolation and rejection can sometimes have a profound place in God's economy.

But having said all this and realizing that loneliness is a valuable and constructive experience in my own life, I still try to avoid these things and protect those close to me from them—for loneliness and rejection are very painful. And I know that they can lead to sickness and the terrors of facing the ultimate issues of

---

*As a matter of fact, some psychologists have discovered that focusing on the fear and the problems involved in doing something risky in one area is often a good way to master fear in another. Thus they discovered that parachuting for some people may be a way of reducing personal fears. Epstein & Fenz, *Journal of Abnormal & Social Psychology* 64 (1962): 97–112.

life—ready or not. Sometimes when our children were small, and one of them felt rejected by a group or thought she was unattractive or unacceptable and felt lonely, my stomach would tighten and I ached for her—I wanted to run and hold my little girls and protect them forever from the pain and rejection of the world. But at such moments I was never sure exactly how to pray. Because every time the situation came up, I remembered a woman named Alice one night many years ago—when I first saw how God could use loneliness and rejection.

We were in a small group of adults who were struggling together to learn how to pray and to live as Christians. We were getting acquainted by going around the room each telling the others some things about his childhood. One older lady had experienced a good many disappointments and seemed bitter about her past. Then it was Alice's turn. She spoke to us hesitantly.

"When I was a tiny little girl, I was put in an orphanage. I was not pretty at all, and no one wanted me. But I can recall longing to be adopted and loved by a family as far back as I can remember. I thought about it day and night. But everything I did seemed to go wrong. I tried too hard to please everybody who came to look me over, and all I did was drive people away. Then one day the head of the orphanage told me a family was going to take me home with them. I was so excited, I jumped up and down and cried. The matron reminded me that I was on trial and that it might not be a permanent arrangement. But I just knew it would be. So I went with this family and started to school in their town —a very happy little girl. And life began to open for me, just a little.

"But one day, a few months later, I skipped home from school and ran in the front door of the big old house we lived in. No one was at home, but there in the middle of the front hall was my battered old suitcase with my little coat thrown over it. As I stood there and looked at that suitcase, it slowly dawned on me what it meant . . . they didn't want me. And I hadn't even suspected."

Alice stopped speaking a moment, but we didn't notice. We were each standing in that front hall with the high ceiling, looking at a battered suitcase and trying not to cry. Then Alice cleared her throat and said almost matter-of-factly, "That happened to me seven times before I was thirteen years old."

I looked at this tall, forty-year-old woman sitting across the room and wept. I had just met Alice, but I found myself loving her and feeling a great compassion for her. She looked up, surprised and touched at what had happened to us as we had responded to her story. But she held up her hand and shook her head slightly, in a gesture to stop us from feeling sorry for her. "Don't," she said with a genuinely happy smile, "I *needed* my past. You see—it brought me to God."

MEMORANDUM

TO: Bruce

FROM: Keith

RE: Chapter One—Loneliness and Rejection

Dear Bruce:

It's really strange, but when I started writing about loneliness and describing it, I felt it again. This time it gave me a chance to think about some of the personal relationships which I've neglected in order to do things like write. I guess loneliness can have lots of uses.

What does loneliness mean to you? I don't believe you've ever told me. Do you see any values in it? Are there some notions regarding loneliness which you think are harmful? What is the conflict in life which you see that drives people into loneliness?

Maybe you could take a shot at some of these either with stuff you've written or thought about.

Keith

P.S. I didn't deal with "rejection" much, except indirectly. Maybe you could talk a little about our fear of it.

In an interview with Dr. Paul Tournier, noted author and counselor, I asked him how he helped his patients overcome fear. His startling reply was that he did not. "What does not frighten, does not have a meaning," he explained; "it's the frightening things which give flavor to life." According to this wise old physician, the right kind of fear is a good and creative thing in a person's life.

For Christians perhaps this thought is not too surprising. The only climate in which faith can grow is one in which there is risk. Having faith is not being without fear. Faith involves trusting enough to risk, even though fear of failure lurks just around the corner.

Many years ago, I heard a brilliant surgeon talking about the gift of pain. "Without pain," he said, "people would not be motivated to find help for very real problems. We should look upon pain as a friend and be grateful for its presence."

Now if fear and pain are forces for good in our lives, what about loneliness? I have no doubt that loneliness and fear of rejection are the most pervasive and serious problems for the greatest number of people in North America today. I meet people of all ages and backgrounds and in every conceivable condition of life wanting help in dealing with their loneliness. Indeed, groups which make a profit preying on this loneliness are thriving. Services, conferences, even advertising campaigns are aimed at the universal problem of loneliness.

Myths about Loneliness

It seems to me there are two prevalent myths about loneliness. *The first myth is that single people are the most lonely.* From my years of privileged listening in counseling situations, I know that most single people seem bitter about their loneliness and tend to feel that if they could just find the right person and marry, their problems would be solved.

I would like to say that I have never heard more intense experiences of loneliness than those described by many of the married people to whom I have listened over the years. Of course, some of these people were married to people whom they had ceased to love or had never loved, and their loneliness is understandable. But it is also possible to be married to the person of your choice—one whom you love—and yet to feel deeply alienated. As a matter of fact, I suspect that the more deeply in love a person may be, the deeper the feelings of loneliness. How many married people wake up at night, watch their sleeping spouse beside them, and are filled with resentment, hurt, and rage? What enormous feelings of loneliness come with thoughts like, *If only he (she) understood me . . . If only he (she) would love me more or in a different way . . . If only he (she) knew the pain he (she) is causing me in this relationship.*

Perhaps the reason loneliness can be more intense in marriage is that a certain hope is gone. The single person can always live in hope that the right person will come along and his lonely vigil will be over. The married person, especially the one who is still in love with his spouse, loses hope because having found his beloved, the ache of being misunderstood or unfulfilled continues.

The second myth about loneliness is that Christians with enough faith should never be lonely. Many Christians believe that while marriage may not solve loneliness, a right relationship to God certainly will. All I can say to add to what Keith has said is that this has not been my experience. Becoming a Christian has not removed fear. I still have fear, but I have a relationship that makes faith grow and makes fear not as destructive as it once was to my relationships and my work. Being in relationship to God has not taken away all my pain, physical or psychic. In the same way, knowing God has not taken away loneliness. As a matter of fact, I don't know of anyone whom I have known deeply who has ever claimed to live a life free of loneliness.

Loneliness as a Gift

I believe that loneliness is basically a gift. It is a reminder of our humanity as Keith indicated. It is the thing that continually drives us to a relationship with God and our neighbor. To take away loneliness would remove the constant motivation to live in fellowship with God and the saints and with our brothers in the world.

When we imply that with enough faith people will never be

lonely, we find ourselves having to live a lie. We feel, *I am the only one who is lonely in this church or in this small group.* When we feel we must hide our loneliness, we deny one of the important motivating and cohesive elements in the building of the Body of Christ.

I believe loneliness is a precious gift because it comes out of our deep humanity and forces us to deal with our original sin of willful separation from God, man, and ourselves. It drives us into relationship. It is a continuing and recurring gift of God to us which makes us strive for an experience within the Body of Christ in which we can be vulnerable and loving with one another.

Openness: A Doorway out of Loneliness

The other day I was driving my motorcycle down a very busy stretch of highway. I was surrounded by cars, with a truck in front of me, a truck behind me and a chain of cars passing me on the left. Just at that moment a wasp flew into my open shirt. (I was not wearing a tie.) Before I could pull off the road several miles later at a convenient, safe place, that wasp had stung me six times on my shoulder, chest, and back. (My wife counted the stings that night.)

However, all the while I was driving along that road with the wasp inside my shirt, I never once did anything but look calm and poised. In the midst of all that traffic, I did not want to appear foolish (any more foolish than I already did as a middle-aged businessman on a motorcycle). I wanted to keep my cool. More important, I did not want to panic the drivers around me who would think they had a crazed motorcyclist on the highway with them.

How many people live their lives with pain or grief, self-hate or guilt, biting them under their psychic shirts. When they keep on smiling as I did on that road, loneliness is inevitable and fellowship is thwarted. Two intensely lonely people who are finally forced to share deeply of love, pain, hope, loneliness and despair have a chance to experience fellowship.

Rejection and Loneliness Related to Fear and Love

Last year I met a wise psychiatrist. He is currently the associate director of a large psychiatric research center and prior to that he ran a statewide mental health program. He had this to say about human relations, "All of life can be boiled down to two basic emotions, love and fear. It's just a matter of people needing people and their love. But because people also get hurt by each other, they are afraid of each other." He went on to say that you can combine these two basic emotions in different ways and build up a tremendously complex system of understanding human relations. But essentially we all need people—we need to love them and be loved by them—and we are afraid of them because we are consistently hurt when we get too close. So, many of us experience a desperate loneliness rather than risk the pain of fear and rejection.

In each relationship, this man says, we are like two porcupines, fearful of getting too close lest we get stuck with the other's sharp quills. But loneliness sometimes provides the "cold night" that forces us to risk getting close enough to survive. The problem seems to be getting close enough to others so that we can survive our universal psychic and spiritual loneliness and yet not be irreparably hurt.

This philosophical psychiatrist said further, "You know, people who come into my office over and over again with the same recurring problems are usually people who cannot find a balance between these two basic emotions. Some feel that because people hurt and reject you, you should avoid them and trust no one. Others have no understanding of reality because they feel that everybody is basically good and you should trust everyone."

I think what my wise friend meant was that learning to cope with a balance of love and fear in relationships is what life is all about. If I say that all people are good and no one will ever hurt me if I trust them, then I must deny and repress the pain that inevitably comes from deep relationships. On the other hand, if I say that everyone is evil and out to hurt me and therefore I should trust no one, I am forced into deadly isolation. We can't live without people and their love and without creative relationships, but at the same time we must be on our guard lest like Abel we unwittingly put our arms around a brother like Cain.

If we avoid deep relationships, we miss the essence of what life with its excitements and challenge is all about. In his book *Tales of Power,* Carlos Castaneda says this about people who fail to cope with the potential of relationship around them. They are like "men for whom an entire life was like one Sunday afternoon, an afternoon which was not altogether miserable, but rather hot and dull and uncomfortable. They sweated and fussed a great deal. They didn't know where to go, or what to do. That afternoon left them only with the memory of petty annoyances and tedium, and then suddenly it was over; it was already night." [3]

Relationships Essential to Transcend Loneliness

Without some meaningful relationships, we are like those men who experience their whole life as a tedious, hot afternoon, and existence has no substance. But rich, creative involvement with others is not guaranteed just because we are Christians involved with other Christians in the church. The Christian *life* is unspeakably more than studying theology, chanting liturgy, being ethical, memorizing the Bible or meeting church budgets. We have Christ's great commandment to "love one another as I have loved you." Since no one can hurt us more than those from whom we expect the most, vulnerable Christian relationships can plumb the depths of potential pain and ascend the heights of potential glory. The more deeply we love, the more deeply we feel pain. But, the more deeply we love, the more we are alive and experience loneliness as a seasoning rather than a pit of despair. In small groups, Christians are rediscovering the adventure of living together—*through* their loneliness has come a new understanding of life.

One of my favorite books is *Zorba the Greek,* by Nikos Kazantzakis. Listen to what Zorba says to his uptight, fearful, proper, English friend, "Boss, life is trouble—only death is not. To be alive is to undo your belt and look for trouble." [4]

To love is to look for trouble and to face the threat of rejection. But to love is to live! And Jesus came that we might have life—together.

Chapter Two

The Inner Life

MEMORANDUM

TO: Keith

FROM: Bruce

RE: Chapter Two—The Inner Life

Dear Keith:
 I'm really excited about getting into this book. But it scares me too, since there are so many changes coming in my life so quickly that I sometimes feel as if there's no place to go apart (to keep from coming apart) to get this book finished.
 The outer world of airplanes, business, speaking commitments and taking care of necessary institutional and material considerations (like paying bills, etc.) gives me the feeling that my body is being jostled through life like an orange bobbling along on a crowded conveyor belt.
 But Martin Buber talks about a private **inner** world of feelings where "life is lived and man recovers from institutions." He points out that as the spectrum of our emotions undulates before our interested glance, like exotic dancers, we can indulge in our likings, our hates and pleasures, and our pain (if it's not too severe). There, inside, we are at home, and we stretch ourselves out in our inner rocking chair, away from the storm of complicated relationships and duties of the marketplace of life outside.
 You told me that you've been learning some new things about the problems of living with yourself and God inside. We've both been through the standard and classical prayer outlines over the years in trying to learn how to love God and do his will. How about writing something about the difficulties of finding God's will through your inner relationship with him.
 Here are some questions I've wrestled with: Are there any objective guidelines to help the average person decide what God's will might be for him? How do you redecorate your inner

space in order to bring Christ in as a Senior Partner? How do you love him? And maybe most difficult, how do you **hear** him? And if that's not enough, how about describing the way you experience your own inner life?

Bruce

It was 5:20 A.M. I woke suddenly without knowing why, about two hours before I'd planned to get up. "Now I am a Christian!" I said it several times. Then I said, "I love you, God," as I lay there totally still in the dim first light of the early morning. But suddenly there clamored onto the stage of my mind like wild animals a dozen intimate fantasies, images, creative plans, ideas, prayers, hopes, sexual feelings, and emotional frustrations. As I looked at these clawing hungry claims on my attention, I found myself fighting off depression and loneliness for no apparent reason.

I was almost overwhelmed by a problem, a kind of warfare no one had told me about when I received the standard list of Christian sins.

My inner life was being reborn for another day. What was I going to *choose* to be the controlling theme of the scenarios which would play themselves out on the inner stage of my mind? For these imaginary dramas provide much of the motivating wind which fills the sails of my behavior. The problem was: how could I find God's will for me in the midst of all these choices?

What Is God's Purpose for Me?

Among the serious Christians I know, there are two notions about where the real action is in doing God's will. Some say it's in helping people by feeding, clothing, and caring for their material needs. They quote Jesus' comment that when you help one of the least of those around you, you are helping him—and this is the mark of those who will get to heaven (Matt. 25:31–46). So they check their behavior with this criterion in mind. Others say there is a prior commitment to helping your brother—that is, keeping your own heart, or inner mind, straight with God—because it is from the heart that outward behavior is born (see Matt. 15:18–20). And if our good works don't come out of conviction from God, this group argues, they are really sin or part of our own ego trip (see Rom. 14:23).

Of course both groups are right. As a matter of fact the Bible, like history in general, is so rich in examples that it seems one can "prove" either side of almost any proposition by a careful selection (and pulling out of context) of specific verses or incidents.

But the Bible with all its richness does not give clear directions about what a Christian should *do* in many of the concrete situations of modern life.

In order to play it safe and avoid the risks of making mistakes while trying to do God's will, many Christians concentrate on a set of negative rules and prohibitions—which, if followed scrupulously, will keep them from the wrath of God.

But Jesus cut right through all the negative, legalistic bindings and sets of rules. When someone asked him what the most significant law was, he gave an answer which forever changed the process of finding God's will: " 'Love the Lord your God with all your heart, with all your soul, with all your mind.' That is the greatest commandment. It comes first. The second is like it: 'Love your neighbour as yourself.' Everything in the Law and the prophets hangs on these two commandments' " (Matt. 22:37–40).

Both—love God and your neighbor! And this dual command was to replace, in the sense of fulfilling, *all* the law and the prophets. But with such a general summary which transcends any list of rules, I wondered how I was going to find out *which specific* course to take each day, each hour.

How can I love God with my whole being and my neighbor as myself when I wake up facing inner fantasies about power, sex, money and possessions, great spiritual conquests, or temptations to feel resentful, depressed, or proud?

Loving God

As I began to try to choose from these fantasies and plans which were the raw materials of my actual motivation for the day, I felt terrible and confused. I realized I'd have to spend some time checking in with God each morning. At first I had a set and structured prayer time in which I learned to "talk to God." And this practice is still helpful. But later I saw that if I were going to get any daily "marching orders," or even specific helpful hints from God, I was going to need a very different kind of "quiet time": one in which I could learn to *hear* God. And that seemed preposterous—though I had often heard Christian speakers say, "I spend at least half of my prayer time listening to God." I didn't believe them. I'd tried it and never heard anything.

How Do You Structure Your Inner Life to Hear God?

Everyone seems to have a "rocking-chair room" in their minds, where they view their fantasies of power, sex, resentment, etc., like closed-circuit TV. They are afraid to let God in that room for fear he will reject them if they consciously share their secret lives with him. But since that is the place of the soul, such fearful Christians have only a formal, wooden prayer life which does not touch the teeming richness of their imaginations—and thus their motivations. Such people sometimes resist a genuine inner life totally or seal off that inner room where their creative fantasies and pleasures dance, and improvise a sort of secluded chapel in their minds (which is much more religious-looking) when they pray.

But this whole problem of hiding from God seems to be the result of the greatest obstacle to the kind of inner life which changes things in the real world: a false idea of God. If I am afraid of God and feel that he is more judgmental than loving, my fear will keep me from letting him or myself be at home in my inner life. And I just won't think about him much.

When I finally saw Jesus in the Gospels as a person with whom tax agents, prostitutes, members of minority groups, social leaders and intellectuals could be accepted and taken seriously, without feeling judged, I began to relax about really letting him in my inner room. I saw that he not only forgave the most blatant sins of people around him, but he built his organization on a friend, Peter, who had failed him three times in one night. As I read these things, I began to relax and tell God what it was really like in my hidden life. This inner relationship and its conversations with Christ became for me the definition of personal prayer.

Right away I saw I'd never be able to love God with my *entire* heart and mind. I often did *not* love him *even* with the conscious part, and sometimes I simply ignored him for days. But then I made a wonderful discovery. Loving God with one's whole mind and heart is a paradox: we can only intend to do it in this life. Lives of the great Christians throughout history attest to this. And the biblical provision for confession and continual forgiveness indicates that although we should not settle for less than total devotion to God, we must face the imperfection of our love and our ambiguous motives if we are going to walk realistically in his adventure.

So I had a new inner "place" where I felt more accepted, just as I was, and there I did not feel any impossible demands to perform or be righteous in order to be accepted by my new inner Companion. But I still didn't know how to understand God's will for the specific choices I had to make each day. What if he had something positive and specific he wanted me to do at a given time? How could I tell what it might be?

Listening to God

For years I had been stumped and just didn't believe that an ordinary person could learn to "hear" God in any specific sense. But then I met Dr. and Mrs. Paul Tournier, the Swiss psychiatrist and his wife. As I got to know them, I asked how they determined God's will for their own lives. They told me that each morning as they prayed together they asked God what *questions* he had for them for that day—*not what answers but what questions.* They would then wait silently for about twenty minutes with a tablet and pencil and write down what came to them. At that point both would share what they had written.

When I first heard this, I was surprised and *very* skeptical. "How do you know," I asked, "that the things you heard and wrote down are not your own veiled or unconscious wishes, and how do you determine which of the many questions that go through your mind are *God's* will for you?"

Paul Tournier said that these dangers were always present and that if a person will not dare to risk being mistaken about the will of God he will never come to know God any better. Evidently it's through obedience, and even misguided actions, that we find greater light—that is, on the condition that we are willing to reexamine our actions afterward quite honestly as if in Christ's presence. God is always the Hidden One who reveals himself only through our groping.[1]

Tournier indicated that prayer is not a static thing for him. It has all the garbled characteristics of life: its directing force, its compulsions, its gropings, its fluctuations, its deviations, its regulating corrections, its growth in volume and strength. What I heard him saying is that when we first begin this listening and writing, we get all sorts of mixed messages from a variety of sources. But if God is real and is trying to communicate with us and we keep listening to him, we will soon be able to hear him better. Besides, by the act of discussing what has come to us with another Christian we can better determine which things we hear are really from God —particularly if both "pray-ers" are also studying the Scriptures.

As Father Andrew pointed out, it's like becoming a trained musician. After a few years of practice and study, one can hear things, right and wrong, which he couldn't hear at first.[2]

So I decided to try this listening with a notebook—asking God what questions he had for me that day. At first I felt strange, sitting there like a secretary with no one else in the room. But then a question formed in my mind: "Why don't you call your daughter?" I wrote it down. And another question came: "Why are you so critical of Harry?" And still another: "Why don't you get back to work writing your book today?" There were others, some with obvious meaning, others seemingly unrelated. But it was a surprising experience. When I called my daughter, I found she really needed help. And as I thought about it, I realized I had been especially critical of Harry and was able to tell him I was sorry. As for the writing project, I became aware that I had been putting it off. It is true these questions may have come from my own unconscious mind, but I can't help but believe they are the kind of questions God would ask me. And they have certainly helped me to know myself and God better and to love people in healthier ways.

I discovered that even apparently unrelated questions often were very close to the problems of doing God's will. For instance I once wrote down, "Why are you so uptight and anxious?" As I looked at the question later I realized that I was anxious and uptight because I was being tempted to do something I knew was wrong. I had repressed the whole situation and hadn't thought I was taking it seriously. But I realized then that I was.

This listening on paper can be done alone, with a partner, or even in a small group. And I have seen amazing and life-changing insights come to people the first time they tried it. On the other hand, some days this listening seems meaningless. But it has been a great help in giving me a sense of specific direction on otherwise chaotic days.

Over the years I have tried many different approaches to communicating with God in my inner life. And to keep the relationship fresh, I believe it is helpful to try different ways of talking, of listening, and of using our imaginations to get to know him better.

I had been falsely led somehow to believe that once I had made a "total commitment" to Christ, my inner life would always be exciting, victorious, and consistent. But although it has been this way sometimes, there are still days of being bored, of doubt, and of outbreaks of inner warfare with God over some very worldly and "unspiritual" issues. But evidently this is the price of growth. I was thrilled to read that Oswald Chambers, that famous exponent of the victorious life, said, "Life without war is impossible either in nature or grace. The basis of physical, mental, moral and spiritual life is antagonism." [3]

It is a peculiarity of human beings that each of us is inclined to feel we are the only one who is divided, tense, anxious, fearful, tempted, and unhappy. But the truth seems to be that most of us who are in touch with our true feelings have our full share of inner problems, regardless of our gifts, knowledge, or experience.

I discovered that when it comes to loving God and one's neighbor, or even one's self, there are only glimpses and brief handlings of grace. According to Pascal, the soul does not lay hold of love or great spiritual achievements. "It only leaps to them, not as upon a throne, but merely for an instant." [4]

But those "instants" can become more frequent and stronger, and can bring a unifying assurance of purpose, presence, and a sense of having an inner "meeting place" in the scheme of things which can never be destroyed.

MEMORANDUM

TO: Bruce
FROM: Keith
RE: Chapter Two—The Inner Life

Dear Bruce:

    As usual I seem to have wallowed around in the feeling aspects of the inner life. And as I look over my stuff for chapter two, I realize I haven't indicated how the inner life ties into outer relationships. Also, I didn't get around to talking about "loving yourself"—as in "love your neighbor as **yourself**."

    Here are some things that occur to me now which I think people might want to know: How do you, Bruce, look at the question of relating to God in the inner life? How do we love ourselves as Christians with all our hangups and hiding? What kind of **language** do you use in your inner dialogue with God? How does God teach us and help us to develop inside?

                                                            Keith

The Inner Life—Two Basic Relationships

The most basic and important relationship is the one which exists between a human being and God. I am convinced that it is impossible to escape this relationship, even if one denies the very existence of a Supreme Being. The people I have known who professed not to believe in God have spent a great deal of time denying him, fighting him, burying him, explaining him away, or attempting to prove others wrong who do believe in him—but any of these enterprises either implies or constitutes a relationship. Perhaps there are those who are totally indifferent to God, who have never given him a second thought, but I have never met such a person.

There seems to be in the make-up of every human being an instinctive sense that Someone or Something is "out there" which cannot be ignored. To some, God is the great unknown; to others, a tyrannical monster; to still others, a quixotic puppeteer who manipulates the universe by pulling strings at random. Actually, a tremendous number of diverse influences play a part in formulating our ideas about God. And it is helpful to remember that our conceptions of God are determined by our training and experiences.

Sometimes people find it hard to believe that God is a loving Father because they are so preoccupied with the laws, rules, and commandments found in the Bible. Standards of ethics and moral laws are not to be confused with the gospel—but in our training and practice they often *are*.

It reminds me of a time when my wife, fed up with the condition in which our children left the bathroom, made this sign and hung it on the inside of the bathroom door: "Do not leave the bathroom until you have cleaned out the washbowl, hung up the towels, put the soap away, and picked up your clothes."

I can't remember that these rules made much of an impact on the behavior of the children, but I do know that some of our guests would come out of the bathroom sheepishly reporting that they had observed all the rules.

This might be a parable of how God has dealt with us. He has given us rules to let us know where we have failed and how we might live if life is to be abundant. But we are not Christians because we keep the rules. The rules point out where we have failed and remind us of the need to respond to God's offer of forgiveness, love, and a new spirit. It is this new spirit which is the fountain for fresh creativity and hope.

Loving Yourself

Second, everyone has a relationship with himself, good or bad. The gospel is good news here, too, for it can mean the end of a certain kind of loneliness, alienation, and separation. For me, the impact of the gospel in this realm—my relationship with myself —has provided an exciting breakthrough. For many years I was afraid to look at myself realistically or to examine the person inside me. I could not classify myself with those who basically like themselves; I was among the vast throng who fear that if we really knew what we were like inside, we would be unable to face the mirror without despising what we saw reflected there.

When Jesus Christ comes to us and affirms us through his own vulnerability, he asks us to become vulnerable—but also to begin affirming ourselves. At least this was my experience. He asks us to affirm ourselves not because we are perfect but because he loves and affirms us. And in the great words of Scripture, "If God be for us, who can be against us" (Rom. 8:31, KJV).

It has made a tremendous difference in my life to realize that I can affirm myself if I really believe in the cross, and will be vulnerable before God, accepting his tremendous affirmation of me in Jesus Christ. If I am really what I claim to be, a sinner in the eyes of God, then I shouldn't be surprised when I fail. At the very moment of failure, I should be able to pray, "Well, Lord, I can't expect much more. As a matter of fact, I'm surprised that I behave as well as I do so much of the time. But now I thank you for pointing out that I have failed and for the conscience that stabs me. I claim your forgiveness, I accept your love, and I will ask my brother to forgive me as I make restitution."

The key is not in covering up our badness, but in facing it quite honestly. The moment we face it, we can believe that Jesus Christ is saying, "I love you now just as much as I loved you when you were performing admirably a few hours or a few days ago."

The Inner Life / 39

Jesus understood our need for self-love. He commanded us to love our neighbor as ourselves. One cannot love his neighbor until he loves himself, so it is tremendously important that we accept the love of God for us in our badness as well as in our goodness.

It was my privilege several years ago to join a group of Americans for a trip to Spain where we met with Dr. Paul Tournier for five exciting days of discussion. One feature of this unusual conference was a workshop for doctors and clergymen involved in counseling. It was a rare opportunity to meet the Christian writer and psychiatrist whose influence has been so widespread.

One of the doctors asked Paul Tournier if it is possible to be a phony Christian. When the question was translated from English into French by our interpreter, Dr. Tournier replied immediately with a whimsical smile, "Mais, oui! C'est moi" ("Of course! It's me").

He then went on to explain that he is often caught in the trap of trying to be something he is not—trying to measure up to the image people have of him, of living up to his reputation, of trying to solve his patients' problems instead of allowing God to solve them.

With a great deal of honesty and charm he talked about the Paul Tournier who is so much like each one of us. The more he acknowledged his own inner phoniness and how unreal he can be at times, the more Jesus Christ was revealed through the life of this man. If he had answered the question with guarded reserve, speaking in general terms about the perils of phoniness, the effect would have been entirely different. By skirting the issue he would have implied that he was Christlike and never phony. But this would have minimized the witness that Christ could make to us through a man who dared to be himself, and who assumed that Jesus Christ would be himself to us when Paul Tournier was being himself.

All of us, even those who know the love of God, tend to become liars when we are left to our own devices. At least this was my own painful discovery. Perhaps this is why Jesus said that where two or three are gathered together in his name, he will be in the midst of us. This is what the Body of Christ is all about. We need one another so that we can be motivated to be honest, and have some measure of objectivity—and even prophetic insight—as we begin to open ourselves.

The gospel is good news not only because of God's unconditional love, but because each of us can join the human race as an odd, unique sort of being.

A few years ago I saw a marvelous piece of communication on a subway wall in New York City. A certain advertising poster showed a very austere, proper, older gentleman recommending a product, and someone—perhaps a little boy writing the dirtiest thing he could think of—had sketched a balloon coming out of the man's mouth containing the words, "I like grils."

Underneath, someone had written with a felt-tipped pen, "It's girls, stupid, not grils."

And below that, in still another handwriting style, someone else had added, "But what about us grils?"

Herein is the marvelous good news of the gospel: when we are honest with ourselves and with a few others, we find that all of us are really "grils"—oddballs and misfits. The gospel is good news for a universal race of those who feel they don't fit in: losers, odd ones, the peculiar, and the out of step—"not the righteous, but sinners."

It is just such people that God loved when he came into the world in Jesus Christ "to seek and save what is lost" (Luke 19:10).

Language of the Inner Dialogue

For many of us, prayer is the natural outgrowth of a new relationship with God and with our inner selves. We want to be in communion with God and sensitive to the promptings of his Holy Spirit. Perhaps, too often we are seeking a spooky or religious experience instead of a direct confrontation with a God who knows us and can speak to us about life as it really is.

I am convinced, as I read the Bible, that God is not very "spiritual" by our usual religious or ecclesiastical definitions. When God intervenes in someone's life, there is a strange lack of "spiritual" language, such as "glory" or "hallelujah" or "praise the Lord."

In speaking to the prophet Jonah, for example, God simply says, "Go to the enemies of your nation and tell them about me and give them a chance to repent and to accept my love and forgiveness" (see Jon. 4).

When God traffics with King David, he sounds very earthy. He convicts David for his irresponsibility about sex, for his dishonesty and lies, and of his need to make restitution (see 2 Sam. 12).

The Inner Life / 41

What did God say to Ananias one morning in Damascus, in the middle of his quiet time, before he was to go off to the sandal factory or wherever he worked? He simply said in effect: "Stop by Straight Street on your way to work and see a man named Saul. He is a prepared person who needs you. I have given you the keys of the Kingdom. Use them to set him free!" The Spirit gave Ananias a specific name and address and commission to stop and see Saul and help him (see Acts 9:10–16). Again, nothing very "spiritual."

When God sent an angel to Peter in prison, the angel kicked Peter awake and gave three simple directions: "Get up; put on your shoes and belt; follow me." He then led Peter out of the prison and disappeared (see Acts 12:1–11).

This, then, is the language God uses to speak to men. He speaks to us, as to David, about our own sins, our need for confession and restitution. He gives us the imperative for specific action: Go! Tell! Help someone! Repay! Get going!

We in the church have been guilty of making the Christian life spiritual in the wrong sense. God is concerned about the specific ways in which our lives are lived out from day to day. The "angel talk" in the Bible is full of verbs and commands to action. We must not retreat into a so-called "life in the Spirit" which ignores the flesh-and-blood world around us. We Christians need more and more to get out of the realm of theological abstractions and into the areas where people are living their lives.

How Does God Teach Us Inside?

When we are open to God's leading, we find that he pushes us into those relationships that threaten us most and in which we feel least comfortable. The Christian life is a dynamic in which no one can say, "I have arrived." Rather, we have begun a life of commitment to Christ in which we find God prompting us to grow and learn and master new skills and establish new relationships.

Many years ago I met a remarkable teacher, one of those gifted people who realizes that she is not teaching subjects but persons. In her classroom young people not only mastered learning skills, but began to understand themselves and life. She was able consistently to encourage her students and help them to excel.

I asked this teacher what her method was. Her reply delighted me and helped me to discover a concept common in education, but new to me, which changed my life and ministry and my understanding of God. She said that it is necessary to be aware of the "growing edge" of each student. The growing edge, it seems, is that area in the student's life where he is ready and able to learn. If you feed him material that he is intellectually or emotionally unable to handle, he is threatened and cannot learn. On the other hand, if you keep repeating things he has mastered, he becomes bored. A good teacher, my friend went on to say, must know what a student *needs* to learn and *is ready* to learn, and then present him with that material.

Surely this is how the Holy Spirit wants to work in each of our lives. Every one of us has an inner spiritual growing edge. We all have mastered certain skills and subjects and disciplines and formed certain attitudes. Our tendency is to sit back and make these the sum and substance of the Christian experience. On the other hand, God says, "Well done," and then moves us on to new areas that we can grasp and master. He urges us toward a life and ministry which will eventually involve our total potential.

Those who are living on the growing edge with God are open to hearing and experiencing things that may seem strange and "unorthodox." At the very point where we dull our growing edge and content ourselves with those things which we have already mastered, spiritual death begins to creep up on us. We all have a tendency to stand still and polish the past. We're like little children who love to have the same familiar stories read to them. They can almost repeat the stories from memory, yet it makes them feel secure and comfortable to hear the words repeated over and over again.

Renewal begins when a person is exposed to the forces that will stretch him and help him to discover the power of Christ in the relationships where he feels least secure. A church discovers renewal when it preaches and acts in a way which motivates the members to move from their own specialties into other dimensions of life.

Several years ago at a pastors' conference, I was having lunch with six other men. Suddenly one young pastor leaned across the table and asked, "Bruce, do you find that you are becoming better as a Christian?"

At first I said, "Oh, yes!" Then, a moment later, "Well, no . . . this is really a very difficult question, let me think for a moment."

The Inner Life / 43

Finally, I told him that while I supposed I was getting better, I certainly was more aware now of areas of disobedience in my life. Also, I had a much greater sense of failure. But I went on to say that the real issue for me lay not in being better or worse, but rather in becoming the person God meant me to be. I am growing in some ways that I would never have dreamed possible a few years ago. God is moving me from my securities into my insecurities, and I am meeting him on the growing edge of my inner life.

Chapter Three

Neighbor-Loving through Dialogue and Listening

MEMORANDUM

TO: Bruce

FROM: Keith

RE: Chapter Three—Neighbor-Loving through Dialogue and Listening

Dear Bruce:

If God's will is for us to love him with all we've got, and our neighbor as ourself, then I think we ought to include some ideas about ways we can learn to love people for Christ's sake. Things move so fast these days that the only contact most people have with others is in "verbal" situations. So let's talk about the nature and effects of conversation itself.

Why don't you put something in about how we can converse with other people in ways that may allow them to feel loved? Without being manipulative, what kinds of things can we say or do which are likely to enable personal dialogue? And how about discussing some of the attitudes which can make everyday verbal exchanges between ordinary people healing and maturing experiences?

Keith

The Art of Conversation

Jesus was the great conversationalist—the master of dialogue. We often think of him as the great physician or the great teacher, but in many of his encounters with people he had no such credentials. Yet the Bible indicates that he began countless ordinary conversations, with amazing results. We have the same opportunity for meaningful conversation in everyday life—on the bus, in the office, at school, in the supermarket.

Many Christians feel they could be more effective with people if they were clergymen, Bible experts, or church officers. But unlike counseling, which takes place between an *expert* and a *seeker,* conversation takes place between *equals.* Some of today's inspired psychologists find that the most meaningful relationships are often established when they meet people as equals rather than on a "professional" basis.

To have dialogue with a gifted Christian conversationalist is a rare and wonderful experience. I will always be thankful for a conversation I had with such a person. He listened to me. He was interested in my struggles, doubts, and hopes. He seemed to understand me. He shared some of the concerns of his own life which were very much like my own. From time to time he asked questions. Finally he prayed with me, not in a condescending way but as a fellow seeker trying to discover God's best. I came away from that conversation a different person.

I am convinced that God intends all Christians to be effective conversationalists. Perhaps this is the highest expression of the priesthood of all believers. People are eager for love and acceptance. Through the art of conversation we can demonstrate that God knows them, loves them, and understands them.

When Jesus spoke with the immoral woman by the Samaritan well, an entire town was affected. She ran into her village announcing that she'd met a man who had told her all there was to know about herself. She did not say this man had raised the dead, or healed the sick, or taught great truths. Yet the town came running en masse to meet him.

Jesus tells us that the things he did we shall do also (John 14:12). The ability to understand people is one of the most effective gifts any Christian can have in the service of his Lord. In each encounter it's helpful to remember that every person is like an iceberg: one-tenth shows and the rest is submerged.

There is a true story about a man who parked his car in front of a supermarket. When he returned, he found the front of his car smashed and no sign of the offending car. His heart sank until he noticed a scrap of paper tucked under the windshield wiper. Opening it, he found this message: "As I am writing this note to you, there are at least sixteen people watching me. They think I am giving you my name and address. Well, I'm not." The point is clear: very often the *obvious* communication is not the *actual*.

People will begin a conversation with trivial things—things which are not threatening. As they trust us more, they may mention the problems of a husband or wife, a child or friend. All the while they may be hoping that we will get at the deeper problems of their own behavior.

We need not consult books on psychology to learn how to recognize revealing signs in people around us. The gift of reading people comes primarily through listening and observing with a lack of self-consciousness. If we cannot read others, perhaps it is because we attach too much importance to making the right impression, or we feel too intensely the need to be loved, admired, or respected. The person who has been justified by faith should not need to impress men or gain their approval. If we believe that God loves us and accepts us as we are, we may be able to begin relating to people more unself-consciously.

Also, if we can relate to people in terms of where they really are, rather than on the basis of their symptoms, we will approach Jesus' own method of dealing with people. For example, most alcoholics have a great need for love. Rather than scolding and shaming them for drinking, we need to supply a relationship of love which gets to the heart of their problem. Self-righteous people who are always impressing us with their good works usually need approval. Those easily irritated are often really saying, "You don't love me enough." The person taking drugs or involved in illicit sex is trying to escape, saying, "I can't stand the hurt of life the way it is."

In Katherine Anne Porter's *Ship of Fools,* one of the characters,

Neighbor-Loving through Dialogue and Listening

a wealthy, self-sufficient divorcée, expresses herself in a bitter but poignant monologue: "Love me. Love me in spite of all! Whether or not I love you, whether I am fit to love, whether you are able to love, even if there is no such thing as love, love me!" [1] When we can hear the sophisticated, the cynical, the hard, the bitter, or the escapist saying this, and can relate to him where he is, we will practice the art of conversation in the way our Lord did.

What Can We Say or Do to Enable Dialogue?

After we have begun to understand another person, what can we do and say and be, in the relationship, in order to enable some kind of meaningful dialogue? Certainly we must identify ourselves as fellow discoverers of the love and power of God. This requires some personal honesty about our own needs and struggles.

Also, we must listen. There is no better way to communicate to a person a sense of his own worth and dignity before God than to listen to the nature and the shape of his struggle.

Along with listening, an occasional question can illuminate for someone his hidden motive, desire, need, or guilt. Jesus' miraculous healing of the Gerasene demoniac began with a question (Luke 8:26–39).

Dr. Robert Sterling Palmer, a Boston physician, in doing a test of four hundred patients, discovered that in many cases asking the right questions produced better results than pills and medicine. The three questions he asked most often were: (1) Do you ever ask yourself what you are getting out of life? (2) Do you ever ask yourself the meaning of life? (3) Do you have a sense of dread or foreboding, panic or terror? As people answered these questions, many tended to discover the psychic and emotional roots behind their physical illnesses.

If a doctor finds that such questions can produce healing more effectively than drugs, then we Christians may be able to use a similar method in our ministry of healing. One doesn't need a medical license to ask questions. Sometimes we need to ask the person what it is he wants most out of life, or what he is dreaming and hoping for. To ask a man about his dreams may give us the privilege of interpreting God to him.

One summer I met a radiant woman, and I asked her about the turning point in her life. She said that several years before someone had asked her, "Does the world need another person like you?" She confessed that at the time she was the gloomiest, sourest, most negative person imaginable. When she replied, "No," and admitted that she really didn't want to be that kind of person either, her friend said, "I think your real name is 'Sunshine.' " Almost from that moment on, the woman became her new name. This kind of life-changing dialogue is all too rare.

Not long ago I read an item in the paper about a tragic incident in Los Angeles: "An unidentified man was killed at dawn today on the Hollywood Freeway after being hit by five cars."

The police said the man was knocked to the pavement by a car which did not stop. He regained his feet and was hit by a second car which also sped off. He got up again and was hit by a third car which sped off. And, believe it or not, he got up once more and was hit by a fourth car which failed to stop. Then, while sprawled on the ground, he was run over by a fifth car.

It's unthinkable that five people could be so callous and uncaring and irresponsible. Yet perhaps this is only an advanced symptom of our time. To a lesser degree, all of us are hit-and-run drivers (or victims) on life's daily freeway.

How many of you have been at a social, professional, or religious gathering where you've spent the evening with a succession of people who seem to run over you with their experiences and convictions and then ricochet off to somebody else? At the end of the evening you feel used, abused, and without a sense of worth. I'm beginning to see that in any encounter, casual or intense, I can be a relational hit-and-run driver on the freeway of life, unless I am conscious of the importance of the other person, listening to him where he is and attempting to have some meaningful dialogue at that point.

Attitudes for Helpful Dialogue

It seems to me there are at least four important attitudes we need to develop as we think about this question of meaningful dialogue.

First of all we need to *believe in the other person's worth.* This is a fundamental attitude that God can give us. If we believe that we have worth, then we can believe that the person we are now involved with also has worth and potential.

A friend of mine is the head of a very flourishing manufacturing company. He is a keen and sensitive person whose life has

Neighbor-Loving through Dialogue and Listening / 51

been changed by God through small groups. Each Christmas he gives his customers and special friends a beautiful art calendar with photographs or paintings of American scenery.

One of these hangs in my office and it reflects my friend Carl's philosophy. Across the top is printed "Created especially for" and in huge block letters, BRUCE LARSON. Then, in very small print, it gives the name of the manufacturing company.

Each time I look at the calendar I know that I am special to my friend and his company. The calendar is not exclusively a means of promoting the name of his company. It says rather that his company knows my name and thinks I'm important.

John Woolman was an amazing Christian who lived in the eighteenth century. He had great passion and zeal, but he also had a gift for dialogue that had far-reaching effects on all of society. Woolman was a Quaker, and at that time many wealthy Quakers were slaveholders. As a young man, he vowed to rid the Society of Friends of this terrible blight, and for thirty years he gave his life to that task.

John Woolman's strategy was basic and unique. He did not picket or hold mass rallies. He didn't publish vindictive sermons against slavery and those who practiced it. Rather, over those thirty years he traveled up and down the length of the land visiting with slaveholders. He would simply accept their hospitality and ask them questions about how it felt as a child of God and a Christian to own slaves. There was no condemnation in his approach. He believed these slaveholders were responsible people of conscience, and he asked them disturbing questions: "What does the owning of slaves do to you as a moral person?" "What kind of an institution are you passing on to your children?"

And so he called forth something noble in the hearts of those Quakers. One hundred years before the Civil War not a single Quaker held slaves. This was the result of one man's social passion coupled with his ability to communicate.

Second, *believe in the other person's future*. Recently I was interviewing the chief clinical psychologist for a statewide research project. He and his staff work with chronic alcoholics or young people who have a terminal illness.

When I asked my friend, "What do you, as a clinical psychologist, think wholeness looks like?" here is what he answered: "I think it has a lot to do with a sort of basic faith in the goodness of life. If I can get the person to face into his life and accept whatever the next day brings with a sense of hopefulness, with a feeling that there is meaning to his experience and his existence and that he is on some kind of a path toward growth, I have succeeded. And, hopefully, that might include some concept of the deity of God.

"And then if he can go at least halfway; make the effort to reach out to life; there is a paradox here—that if he will take responsibility for himself and his decisions and where he is . . . if he just reaches out toward life—just to meet the fundamental responsibilities—things will unfold for him. I know that's a very weird description, but that's what I'm into these days. It's really strange."

I couldn't believe my ears. This gifted, trained psychologist realizes that he has no greater gift to give others than to believe in them and their future. To have hope for them means that they will begin to discover their own hope and to claim it.

I suppose this underlies almost all effective work with people at any level. I recently heard of an inner-city, integrated church that was absolutely brim full at every service and where people were finding help and hope and change. The pastor was asked the secret of his ministry. "Oh, it's no secret," he said. "I simply tell people who they are!"

Ideally every pastor ought to be able to do this in the pulpit and every parishioner should be able to tell the people around him the potential he sees in them. All of us Christians ought to be able to tell people who they are and to have hope that the great days are ahead and to live in that kind of personal, positive eschatology.

Third, *believe in the other person's possibilities*. Don't feel it's all up to you.

I attended a Bible study recently, and the teacher was talking about the conversation in Genesis 4 between Cain and God. Cain had just killed his brother Abel and God asked him, "Where is your brother?" Cain answered, "I do not know. Am I my brother's keeper?"

The teacher went on to say that in the Bible the Hebrew word for "keeping" always refers to animals, *never* to people. So when Cain responds to God about "keeping," he knew that he was not meant to be in the business of "brother keeping." And yet, so much of our theology about relationships has to do with "brother keeping." "Brother keeping," as seen from this perspective is always patronizing. It puts one person in a superior position to

Neighbor-Loving through Dialogue and Listening / 53

another. It makes one the giver and the other the receiver, whether of food, money, or advice.

Father Damien, a Roman Catholic priest, served for years by his own choice in the leper colony of Molokai in Hawaii. He customarily began his Sunday morning sermons with the words, "My brothers and sisters." But on the Sunday after he contracted leprosy, he began with "We lepers . . ." Until that week he had led as one who had come to help lepers, but now his ministry was different. From that point on he was locked in and irrevocably committed to his congregation. They were equals. And amazing things began to happen in the lives of the other lepers.

Finally, *believe in the other person's judgment.* How much we need to practice this in all our relationships.

One church has adopted a new rule for all official board meetings. No one is allowed to speak against another person's recommendation until he has said three good things about it. What a marvelous rule that would be for every family, every committee, every staff. First affirm the other person's judgment by saying three good things about his suggestion or recommendation. After that you are permitted to give reasons why you might be against it. Obviously there are some recommendations for which it may demand some creative thought to come up with three affirmative statements.

But to oppose a person's suggestion immediately, even though your reasons are sound, is to say to that person that he is stupid and that he doesn't count.

A cartoon I saw recently portrayed an executive presiding at a staff meeting. This very pompous man with a scowl on his face is saying to his colleagues around the conference table, "The report is, of course, largely my work. But I don't want that to inhibit you. Run through it with a fine-tooth comb. If you find any flaws, don't hesitate to speak up because, make no mistake, this report will affect us all. I don't intend doing anything childish like putting it to a vote, but anyone not in favor should stand up now so that we can . . . *see his stupid face!*" [2]

How often I have responded (a little more subtly) in just that smug, superior, put-down way to friends, colleagues, my children, my wife. Frequently, our own attitudes about others' abilities keep them from being able to share themselves and their humanity with us.

The greatest gift you have to give is yourself—but on a par with giving yourself is giving your acceptance of others as first-class human beings. And when we give ourselves *with* our acceptance, amazing kinds of healing and growth can be born out of our dialogue with people.

MEMORANDUM

TO: Keith

FROM: Bruce

RE: Chapter Three—Neighbor-Loving through Dialogue and Listening

Dear Keith:

Last night on the phone I was intrigued by your ideas about how listening is related as a necessary prerequisite to giving yourself and loving, and why the act of listening may be so powerful. Why don't you put some of that on paper for this chapter.

Also, in my material I suggested the need for more openness in Christian dialogue. How about developing that a little—like how honest should we be? Where and how does a Christian learn to relate more honestly? And what happens if someone gets mad or threatened in a dialogue or group situation?

                                                                             Bruce

Listening, Giving, and Loving

My mother had dropped the antique crystal container for her face powder. It had shattered into a thousand pieces, and she had cried. Being five years old, I was impressed and saddened to see my mother crying. I listened as she told me its history. And I tried to comfort her. Her birthday was that week, and I remember taking all my pennies out of my secret hiding jar. Without telling anyone where I was going, I walked from our house on the edge of town clear to Main Street (which was probably about a mile and a half). I went to the five-and-ten and blew my entire savings—about nineteen cents—on a cheap blue glass powder bowl with regular glass bumps all over it. I then walked home and gave it a super five-year-old's birthday wrapping. At supper time I put it by my mother's plate.

When she got through the dirty fingerprints to the present and found out what I'd done to get it, she held me tightly to her and cried more than she did when she first broke her crystal bowl. I was confused—but I sure knew I'd done *something* right about letting her know I loved her.

Only very recently did I realize what had happened. Out of my listening and watching I had seen another person's hurt, and I had given all I had at the time to try to relate specifically to what had gone wrong. This combination constituted giving *myself* in a tangible way. Unfortunately, most of the rest of my life I have not listened and watched first and then offered myself with the gifts I've given people close to me. Instead, I have usually bought what *I* would have liked—and not heard the other person's needs and wants. Consequently I have been disappointed when the recipients didn't respond with my mother's gratitude—which is of course a sign that I was giving to meet my need rather than their needs. I was expecting the gift to call attention to me. Realizing this recently has been especially painful, since my wife is the best selector of gifts to fit the person I've ever known.

But through this realization I have learned that listening is a prerequisite to almost any kind of effective giving or expressing of love.

What Does Listening Do?

I remember Bruce's saying once that in a counseling situation "interested listening" by a therapist is experienced by the client as love. So listening by itself would be of great value. And the reason listening is experienced as love is probably because it is a profound affirmation of the worth of the person being listened to. If you really listen to me you are telling me nonverbally that I am worth your time, that what I have to say is not meaningless (and thus I am not meaningless), and that is very affirming to me. This simple affirmation is *very* important in keeping me balanced, because, as Reuel Howe has said, "Our life situation is one in which we are always seeking affirmation, and if we do not receive it, we try to provide it for ourselves." [3] And in our fear of rejection—of not being recognized as valuable—we often do bizarre things or avoid relationships and situations in which we might be rejected, thus avoiding opportunities to be loved.

One of the carry-overs of this fear of rejection in my life is that even now when I enter a room filled with people, many of whom I am supposed to know, I will lock eyes with someone across the room and with jovial expression and hand outstretched go straight to him or her to avoid the contacts with the eyes along the way—thus avoiding the possibility of forgetting a name or face and possible rejection.

But I began to realize that as a Christian who wanted to know and love my neighbor, I was going to have to learn to listen to him, to try to hear his hopes and his hurts. I saw that this sort of affirmation is only really effective if it is authentic and if it springs out of a genuine interest in the person and a knowledge of what he is like. And this kind of relating feels like the action of love—because it *is*.

The whole world out there is crying out for love and affirmation from other people—from someone of significance. This is really the outer side of a deeper need—the need for *self*-acceptance. But how can we help someone understand and love himself? Carl Rogers feels that no one can understand and love himself as he is until *another* first understands and accepts him for what he is. So listening not only makes people feel loved and affirmed, but it makes them feel *understood.* And if they feel understood, they may begin to understand themselves and see their true needs and worth to God. Then the gospel may become believable.

For years I felt as if I should "help" people with my responses after listening to them pour their hearts out. I guess this is because I have been trained to be a "leader" and "counselor." And yet I find that most of my formal training in psychology and theology simply is not effective in trying to relate to another person in an honest way as a brother in Christ. For example, in graduate school I was trained to maintain a professional detachment so as not to get sucked into the other person's problems. The theory was that if you let a drowning man get his hands on you, you'll both likely go under. And I hasten to add that in some cases this is true. But I think we have gone too far in our detachment.

Jesus' Kind of Involvement

But one can listen only so long. Then a response of some kind is called for or the listening is not consummated. What kind of response can bring people closer to God and each other?

As Henri Nouwen put it: "After so much stress on the necessity of a leader to prevent his own personal feelings and attitudes from interfering in a helping relationship . . . , it seems necessary to re-establish the basic principle that no one can help anyone without becoming involved, without entering with his whole person into the painful situation, without taking the risk of becoming hurt, wounded or even destroyed in the process. The beginning and the end of all Christian leadership is to give your life for others. Thinking about martyrdom can be an escape unless we realize that real martyrdom means a witness that starts with the willingness to cry with those who cry, laugh with those who laugh, and to make one's own painful and joyful experiences available as sources of clarification and understanding." And of course he's right. For "who can listen to a story of loneliness and despair without taking the risk of experiencing similar pains in his own heart and even losing his previous peace of mind? In short: 'Who can take away suffering or loneliness without entering it?' " [4]

Being Friends in Christ

But I realized that this approach of sharing parts of one's inner life is not a matter of "leading" or "ministering" but of being a *friend* in *Christ*—that the vulnerability which is so necessary in a helping relationship can become the *normal style* for Christians in their living together. In other words, the natural involvement through listening and revealing ourselves to each other can bring love, healing, and genuine life-giving affirmation to us. But *also,* in this process of creating and sharing personalness we will unconsciously become trained to bring love, healing, and affirmation to our neighbors in the world.

The Nature of Honesty in Christian Friendship

Some people have thought I was stating that personalness is created by a raw and uninhibited honesty *about other people* and their behavior. But I am saying that one begins deep Christian dialogue and friendship with a vulnerable honesty about *himself* and his own feelings and behavior.

In the small-group movement there seem to be two distinct approaches to breaking through people's façades. It's almost as if we were chickens trapped in our shells. One way to break the shell is with a hammer. Some psychologists have found uninhibited confrontation very effective with tough shells. But an untrained lay leader may have some crippled and helpless chicks on his hands. The other way to make contact with the person inside is to create an atmosphere of safety and warmth (through confession) in which the chicken can come out from the inside at his own speed. The ratio of healthy chicks seems higher. And this is the approach of most of the small groups with which I've been associated.

The Terror of Beginning

But in my journey, I find truly vulnerable honesty with other people to be very difficult. At first I was only honest with God in the privacy of my prayers. I was still afraid that if *other* Christians knew what I was thinking in my inner rocking-chair room they wouldn't accept me—just as I always suspected that if anyone got close enough to *really* know me, they would walk away and leave me. But then came a miracle. One day in a counseling situation, in order to identify with a man who was really suffering from guilt, this inner honesty accidentally spilled over into my outer life.

The man confessed a problem in a close relationship which reflected an attitude he definitely considered to be un-Christian. He was a very sensitive person, and his rejection of himself for having these feelings was intense. After his confession I looked at him for a long minute; he seemed so lonely with his problem—and I was horrified to realize that I had the *same difficulty that morning*. I was tempted to pray for him and keep still about my problem. Actually I just wanted to get away. But since I couldn't, I found myself sort of sheepishly telling the man in his misery that I experienced the same kind of jealousy and hostile resentment he had *that same day*.

I thought he would walk out of my office in disgust. But instead, he just looked at me with great relief, and then thanked me. I remember being very surprised at his reaction and realizing that he hadn't primarily wanted an exalted counselor "answer man." He had wanted someone more like a friend to be *with him* in his problem. And my identification with him as a "sinner" was a kind of "answer" from his perspective—since we were *side by side* before God in need of grace and forgiveness. Somehow, for that moment, we were both freed. And I had a glimpse of what relatedness in God's Kingdom could be.

Finding Some Friends to Learn With

This Christian friendship does *not* necessarily mean *confessing one's most awful sins*. Total confession is a special kind of relationship which may or may not develop out of the sort of friendship I'm describing. And as Paul Tournier says, one should choose his "confessor" out of a thousand. But not so his open Christian friends. Here, in sharing our lives we can learn to be natural and vulnerable about the activities of our inner minds a little at a time, as the relationship grows.

Also this being more open does *not* mean that one should feel compelled to tell his feelings to a friend or in a group. The need for privacy is very important and should be respected. And besides, a person is not free unless he can choose when he will speak, what he will reveal, and when he will be silent. Christian friends can tell each other what they do and do not feel ready to reveal. And the boundaries of their freedom will almost undoubtedly grow as time goes on. As a rule, I have found it best to be as open as possible without trampling other people's privacy—including my family's.

As I indicated earlier, it seems to me that this process itself is perhaps the best training for being friends in Christ to the people "in the world." I believe that this is the meaning of Luther's daring statement that we are to become Christ for each other—to love and receive love and forgiveness in his name.

The Breaking Point of Dialogue

But there will come a crisis point in this process of being friends in Christ—between individuals and in groups. After the first flush of warmth and gratitude at being accepted—there comes a time when friends disagree or when one hurts the other. Many of us are so afraid of losing the love of a friend that we run back to our masks of isolation, shallowness, and safety in terror rather than confess our hurt, anger, or disagreement. And when one side of a two-way exchange dries up, the other does too. When this happens, Christians may continue to call themselves friends, but the nourishment which keeps friendship and love growing dries up.

The development of a friendship or group may also break down because one person may have a terror of being revealed and rejected when the dialogue reaches a certain depth. So he will block the relationship with unanswerable, intellectual questions or with silence or seemingly unreasonable attacks. And everyone else gets defensive, anxious, and hostile, not realizing the threat the group's progress suddenly presents to one member.

At such times the only way I have found to restore personalness is for both parties (or the group) to stop and tell exactly what they are *feeling* right at that moment. For instance, in the middle of a terrible argument, I once said, "Wait! I'm feeling hurt and put down as a person and I'm wanting to hurt you. What are you feeling?" The other person answered, "I feel left out, as if you do not think I'm intelligent and I want to shout at you to pay attention to me." I never would have guessed that reaction from the person's apparent confidence and the strength of his blast at me. Suddenly we were out of the realm of attack and counterattack and back to our inner lives where our only hope of Christian dialogue lay.

I guess I am finding that the structure and timing of when to "listen" or "pray together" or "share the word" are not nearly as clear-cut and well defined as I once thought. The most touching witness of the Holy Spirit's presence in a dialogue might be a tear or cry from the "stronger" Christian or a burst of laughter from one who is dying of cancer. It is the sharing of *reality* with other people in the presence of Christ's spirit that has made me feel at home and loved in God's family.

But as one begins to share his inner life more openly, a strange thing may happen. It is as if we discovered a small thread coming out of the corner of our mouth as an innocuous unrevealed thought. And as we pull the thread out and are accepted, we discover that it is tied to a string—a more threatening truth about ourselves. To the string is tied a rope and then a large chain. We fear that at the end of the chain is a bucket of garbage which, if it ever came out into the light of anyone's presence, would cause us to be rejected. Of course, for most people this will never happen.

But at some point a Christian may feel a need to "get it all out" before God. If so, how does one find a place to dump his most rotten spiritual and emotional garbage? But that question leads to the whole matter of confession—its advantages and dangers.

Chapter Four

Confession

MEMORANDUM

TO: Bruce
FROM: Keith
RE: Chapter Four—Confession

Dear Bruce:
   I closed the last chapter by asking where one might go to confess his deepest and most private sins. Since some people do not understand either the background or the need for this sort of confession, how about giving a little history of confession and describe what goes along with the act of confessing? You might put something in about the benefits of confession and the penalties of being closed—and anything else which seems important to you.
   As I've told you before you've helped me in this area more than anyone else (although I thought you were a real fanatic when I first heard you talk about "confessing before a brother").

                                                     Keith

Some years ago, I pulled into a gas station to ask directions. I was looking for a meeting of young people where I was to lead a workshop. I bought some gas, and as I gave the attendant my credit card, I said, "I'm lost." Noticing that my credit card was marked "Reverend," he smilingly said, "Ah, I see you're a clergyman. So you're not really lost like most of us."

"Oh, but I am," I replied. "Being a clergyman doesn't mean that you can't be lost in some of the most basic areas of life. It just means that you ought to know where to go for help." The man shook his head; he would not and could not believe that a clergyman could be as lost as he was.

This is a parable of many people in the church. We might be lost, but we can't believe that a fellow Christian or fellow church member or fellow deacon or elder or fellow women's association officer could be like us, and so we live as part of a conspiracy of silence and we die for the lack of real communication and the help that God could give through confession of our lostness and of our sin.

History of Confession

It's interesting to trace the history of confession in the Christian church. The church, of course, officially began at Pentecost after our Lord's death and resurrection, with the coming of the Spirit. But the foundation for the church as we know it was laid by our Lord's own life and ministry and his relationships with his disciples and the people of Palestine. During his three years of ministry Jesus must have been a very open person. How else could we know about his temptation in the wilderness? No other human being was there. How would we know about his discouragements, his sorrows, his fear of the cross, his agony before God as he wrestled with the Father's will? We know about them only because our Lord himself disclosed them to faithful men who passed them on to us.

After the church was born at Pentecost, we find a little society meeting in homes, basements, caves, catacombs, and quickly multiplying all over the inhabited world. For the first four hundred years we know through historical record that Christians practiced confession in the fellowship. When someone committed a sin, it was shared openly in the entire worshiping congregation.

Then as the church grew, it became both embarrassing and difficult for everyone to be honest with everyone else in his particular congregation of believers, his branch of the company of the committed. So with the emergence of persons designated as clergy, and with the growth of the church, the public method of confession became optional. A believer had the choice of confessing to a clergyman or priest privately or in the fellowship of the church. But by the thirteenth century, as worship became more formal, we find that confession was sealed off from the fellowship and was from then on heard only by a priest. Some time later the Protestant Reformers, trying to discover the roots of authentic Christian life and to recapture the power of the early church, talked about the priesthood of all believers. This was largely interpreted to mean not that every Christian was a priest to his brother, but that no Christian needed a priest because we had Christ. Confession to a brother was a rarity. But over two hundred years later, a great deal of the power of the Methodist revival evidently came from Wesley's small groups in which confession to the group was an essential feature.

From that time until the present, the power of the church has tended to diminish as confession became less public and more private. Simultaneously mental and emotional illness has grown and, in point of fact, has taken such a giant step that psychosis is one of the primary illnesses of our time. I cannot help but feel there is a connection between the growth of mental illness and the sealing off of the confessional.

Today, almost no one doubts the need for confession. All of us live with a tremendous amount of guilt. I suppose it's always been true but, in these times especially, we are faced with many everyday choices that leave us with guilt. Picture a man who has promised his wife that he will spend the evening with her, since for many nights he has been away on all kinds of civic and church work. Just as he is leaving his office, he meets a friend in need of a listening ear. He then has to decide whether he will renege on his promise to his wife or leave a brother in possibly serious trouble. I am suggesting that there is no way out of that dilemma without feeling real guilt. To live outside of a monastery entails living with real guilt. Or, perhaps life in a monastery is even more guilt-producing because it is so physically removed from the hurts and needs of the secular world. The Christian does not leave his guilt behind him. A guided life does not produce a guiltless life. Learning how to deal with guilt is the heart of the matter.

Dealing with Guilt

Helping people to deal with their guilt is part of our ministry as Christians and involves this confessional dimension of life. In the Book of Acts (chap. 9), when the risen Lord confronts the Apostle Paul (at that time called Saul) on the road to Damascus, Paul's life is not immediately changed. Rather, he is led into Damascus, miserable, his life tumbled in, sick, blind, and unable to eat. Three days later a layman named Ananias walks in, sent there because of his dialogue with God during his morning quiet time. It's at the hands of Ananias that the power of the Holy Spirit falls upon Paul. His sight and his health are restored, and he becomes a new being in Christ.

And what happened between Paul and Ananias? In all likelihood Paul was able to open up his heart and talk about the Christians he had killed as a result of his well-meaning zeal. He probably also talked about other mistakes in his life. Ananias was not only Paul's confessor, but he could pronounce absolution in the name of Jesus. He could pray with Paul and see God's healing come.

Several years ago I received a letter which was sent to two other men as well. In part this is what it said:

Dear Bruce and Frank and Jack,
 I am sending a copy of this letter by way of greeting to all three of you. You have all meant so much to me and I have procrastinated too long in telling you what has happened. [There follows a description of his wife's emotional and mental illness and how he finally got in touch with the doctor she was seeing, a clinical psychologist.] The doctor's theory is based on openness and the ability to admit to the significant others in our lives the exact nature of our wrongs. I was John Smith, though. I had been to three Christian conferences and I had committed my life to Christ, admitting one thing that had been wrong.

Beyond that, I couldn't have any wrongs because I had been saved. I got to talk to this doctor after lunch and I found out some of my wrongs. [He then lists several sins he shared with the doctor.] Then the doctor asked about money. I said, "Yes, I took ten or fifteen cents out of our cash register at dad's store a lot of different times." The doctor then asked about now, and I said, "Oh, nothing." Then I started to think. It was pretty easy to forget to ring up some of the checks that came in and have the extra money around to make me look like a big shot, and then it just got to be a habit and so much was channeled out monthly. The doctor then asked if there was anything else and I said I didn't think so. He then wanted to know if I was willing to go in and tell the group therapy people these things. I said yes, and I did. The group gave me strength, certainly not in approving of what I'd done but helping me bear the burden. They asked if my wife knew of this and I said no, I didn't think so. And I went to my wife and told her all.

A couple of weeks later I found myself back in the group, telling my story again. One of the people in the group mentioned something about restitution. I wasn't taking money any more, but paying it back had never occurred to me. My wife helped me to see that I had to tell the authorities. So I went to my C.P.A. and told him my story and how much had been withheld. What it amounted to was that I owed money plus interest to the Internal Revenue Service for income tax. The C.P.A. went back and refigured the tax returns for the eight years involved, and we made a voluntary disclosure to the Internal Revenue Service. It cost me close to one thousand dollars in interest for my stupidity. I was then able to go to the significant others in my life and tell my wrongs. . . .

[Further on in the letter, as he is about to close:] Once I had cleaned my clothes, I was in a better position to help my wife. She seems to have made more improvement lately.

It seems to me that my friend's therapist played a role not unlike that of Ananias in his encounter with Paul. Unfortunately, he did not find this basic kind of help in his church or in the Christian conferences he attended. It was at the hands of a secular psychologist in a secular group that God was able to bring in the dimension of the confessional and bring about restitution, which has made him a whole and free person. In the church we are seldom able to tell others where we have failed, let alone be encouraged to make restitution.

I feel great admiration for the Roman Catholic church which for two thousand years has clung tenaciously to this dimension of the confessional as a part of the cure of souls and of helping people to become new. And they have made this available for all of their members. Those of us in the Reformed tradition had to wait for Freud and psychoanalysis to discover man's need to deal with his guilt. We are in debt to these apparently incongruous streams—the Roman Catholic church and psychoanalysis. For, while each has mistrusted the other, they have kept alive this source of healing to guilt-ridden people.

Confession and the Power to Minister

When I gave my life to Christ, my direction changed. I began to study more, to be caught up in doctrine and theology. But for years after my conversion, I found that I was still ineffective. I was unable to love myself, to love others, to relate. I was justifying myself. And all this behind the façade of being a Christian.

The real turning point came at a meeting in New York where people of all denominations and colors and creeds and conditions were learning how to be open and honest with one another, or, as they called it, "to walk in the light." It was in this crowd that I discovered the difference between forgiveness and cleansing. I had claimed the forgiveness of Christ on the cross years before, over in Germany after World War II. I knew that I was forgiven and that I lived as a man who was forgiven. But the Bible speaks about confessing your sins one to another so that you might be healed (Jas. 5:16). It goes on to say that "If we confess our sins, he is faithful and just to forgive us our sins, and to cleanse us from all unrighteousness" (1 John 1:9, KJV). As I opened my life to another friend, I found the power of God and the cleansing of God, even as Paul must have found it on Straight Street in conversation with Ananias.

The Gospels are full of this power that God releases through the confessional. Look what happened to Zacchaeus when Jesus, passing through town, came to have dinner with him. We can see the two men probably alone in Zacchaeus's dining room. Suddenly, Zacchaeus opens his heart and begins to tell Jesus how he got his money and how he used people, and eventually he promises to make amends. At the end of their meal Zacchaeus has found such newness of life that Jesus says, "Today salvation has come to your house" (Luke 19:1–10, RSV).

I have often heard Paul Tournier say that the turning point for him regarding his freedom to minister was not his conversion. For years he was a Bible-believing, church-going, converted Christian, but without effectiveness or power. Then one day in New York he went to a small meeting in a home where people were simply being themselves, sharing deeply of hurts, joys, sins, excesses. It was in this climate that Tournier became new. When he returned to Geneva and his medical practice, he suddenly found people opening up to him. Instead of talking only about their physical symptoms, patients began to talk about their lives and Tournier turned into the amazing counselor he is today.

I believe everyone needs a confessor, because our basic sin is pride. That which keeps us from being in a real and open relationship with God and one another is usually not our sin but our pride in not revealing our sins. As Christians we believe that Christ died for our sins, but if I cannot tell my brother about my sin which has been forgiven, that can make me unreal and phony with him. The Bible speaks much about this and about the fact that our real sin is self-justification.

Take, for example, two men in the Bible who demonstrate two radically different ways to handle sin. One is King David and the other is Moses' brother Aaron. One is a liberator of men and the other is a roadblock to God's purposes. One man is full of joy, abandon and grace; the other man is reluctant, dragging his feet, full of questions and regrets. The difference between these two men is not in their goodness, for both have sinned. It is not even in the degree of sin, though David is by human standards, I suppose, a greater sinner than Aaron. David is an adulterer, a thief, a liar, and a murderer. But these two men deal with their guilt very differently. When David is nailed again and again by God through people or circumstances, he is quick to admit to God and to his fellowmen that he has sinned, to make restitution, and to believe that he is loved by a God who will and does forgive. (See 2 Sam. 12; 24; Ps. 51.)

Aaron, on the other hand, denies his guilt. When Moses comes down from the mountain, having talked with God, and sees the people dancing before a golden calf instead of worshiping God, he rightly blames Aaron. But Aaron says, "I don't know what happened. We didn't make any calf. We simply threw all of our gold utensils and jewelry into the fire and out came this calf." (See Exod. 32:15–24.) Aaron had to try to justify himself and so missed God's forgiveness while David could confess his sin and therefore could experience grace.

The Consequences of Closedness

Because the Reformed part of the church has been so unwilling to take the need for confession seriously, we find psychology taking the lead. The new psychology, which is really a revolt against some of the Freudian emphases, treats emotional disturbance by helping people to accept responsibility, or blame, for their problems. Under the Freudian system, responsibility for failure was often placed on parents, friends, wife or husband, all those who allegedly treated the patient badly. The new psychology views the individual himself as the one who is basically hiding his guilt and refusing to take the blame. These new psychologists consider the neurotic and even the psychotic a person who has a fairly well-developed superego that is not quite strong enough to keep him from yielding to temptation. After he succumbs, the individual's conscience begins to bother him. He starts hiding his deviant acts from others, and, in order to hide, he must lie. And in order to cover up one lie, he has to tell more lies. So the first step in this chain of illness leads to a neurosis and to the kind of behavior which leaves him socially vulnerable. He becomes more and more secretive, seclusive, and cut off from all the world around him.

These new psychologists believe that this self-inflicted secrecy encourages illness and prevents healing. The patient is afraid that someone is going to find out about him, so he continually leads a guarded life, one marked by anxiety and the dread of exposure. The more he hides and conceals, the less he is able to share intimately with others and the less he dares to have any meaningful contact with other people. He sometimes tends to become an authority in subjects so that he can speak, preach, teach, or lead and thereby avoid any kind of intimate relationship. Ultimately, he deliberately avoids any attempt to relate, even to members of his family, his peer group, or his community because relating to others has become so threatening. He becomes a closed person.

Men like Hobart Mowrer who have been leading in this new psychology believe that there are only two paths available to such a closed, alienated person. He can reveal his real self and become an open person, or he can start believing his own lies and begin more completely to inhabit his unreal world. The second alternative often leads the neurotic into the typical syndromes of schizophrenia. The world of delusions and hallucinations becomes the real world, and the world of reality becomes unreal.

Walking in the Light—a Source of Strength

Hopefully, the new church is a society of those who "walk in the light." Walking in the light means living without a bag full of secrets. Your motives, your attitudes, your decisions are shared quite informally through the course of the week in the many situations in which you find yourself with other Christians. To be a part of a small group of people who live this way can be one of the most challenging and liberating experiences that I know.

Pope John XXIII brought this dimension to the entire Christian world. He was a walking confession, a real man who was also a Christian, who was also the pope. After being elected pope, one of his first acts of office was to visit one of the large jails in Rome. As he was there giving the prisoners his blessing, he told the men that the last time he had been in jail was to visit his brother. What a breath of fresh air! The pope, considered by many to be Christ's vicar on earth, came from a real family and knew what it was to share the hurts and joys of all men everywhere.

The meaning of the phrase "walking in the light" came to me many years ago on a Pennsylvania highway near Scranton in the middle of the night. As I was driving along, I took the wrapper off some candy and, finding the ashtrays in the car full, I opened the window and threw it out. Suddenly I realized that I would never have done this in the daylight. Somehow, the very darkness encouraged me to litter, a thing I deplore. Daylight, on the other hand, reminds us of our responsibility to other people and helps us to do the responsible thing.

People who do not live in fellowship with others live in perpetual darkness and continually do things of which they are ashamed. But people who live in a fellowship where they know and are known are more likely to live in the light and are encouraged to be and to do those things of which they can be proud.

I know that many people are concerned that this kind of confessional fellowship might overfocus on the negative. François

Fénelon lived between 1651 and 1715. He faced that problem in his day, and his word is a good word for us today, as an ancient Christian to contemporary Christians.

> As light increases, we see ourselves to be worse than we thought. We are amazed at our former blindness as we see issuing forth from the depths of our heart a whole swarm of shameful feelings, like filthy reptiles, crawling from a hidden cave. We never could have believed that we had harbored such things, and we stand aghast as we watch them gradually appear. But we must neither be amazed nor disheartened. We are not worse than we were; on the contrary, we are better. But while our faults diminish, the light by which we see them waxes brighter and we are filled with horror. Bear in mind, for your comfort, that we only perceive our malady when the cure begins.

Forgiveness

As we see more of our true selves, it is difficult to believe that Christ loves us *just as we are*. We are impatient, grumpy, irritable, nagging, fault-finding at home or in the office or in school, because many of us really hate ourselves. It is difficult to believe that right now, in the light of what we have just done, God loves us as much as he says he does. When I find myself critical of people I live with at home or work, I don't need more patience but time alone to let God remind me of his love for me. When I know that I am loved by him and am forgiven for present failures, then I find that the things which have been so irritating in my family members or colleagues become trivial. We must learn to take the cross seriously and experience day by day and moment by moment Christ's overpowering love and forgiveness, not only for sins past, but for sins present. He does not say to us, "Change, that I might love you." As we read the biblical record of Jesus talking with people, we sense his total love for them as they are. This love motivates them to change. We do not repent *in order* to be loved, but *because* we are loved by him.

Finally, "If the Son . . . shall make you free, you shall be free indeed" (John 8:36, KJV). We must not repress feelings that are wrong but let them come out where God can deal with them. We tend to think that being a Christian is to pretend love for those whom we do not love, smiling meekly to hide the churnings inside.

"Telling somebody off" is not the best way, but it is often healthier than pretending nothing is wrong.

We Christians have a wonderful promise, "There is therefore now no condemnation for those who are in Christ Jesus" (Rom. 8:1, RSV). We must try to be ourselves, in love, believing that Christ loves us as we are and does not condemn us. "If we confess our sins, he is faithful and just to forgive us our sins. . . ."

MEMORANDUM

TO: Keith
FROM: Bruce
RE: Chapter Four—Confession

Dear Keith:
Enclosed is my part of chapter four. Attempting a book like this is crazy. Here we are taking some of the most difficult questions which face Christians and treating them with ten-page half chapters. But maybe it's a beginning.

Keith, you have cautioned me several times about how frightened people are of being exposed. Since I already know that, I sometimes get a little irritated with you. But I also know you are saying something important—that we should beware of **pushing** people into vulnerability. You've told me that your own journey toward private confession was a gradual and scary one. How about writing something about it here—at least some of the parts about hiding feelings and sins; moving from general to specific confession to God, then before another person. What are some of the things which keep us from confessing? How does it feel to take the risk? And how about confessing in groups?

(If you need more suggestions, don't hesitate to write.)

Bruce

Confession of Need

Confession means more things for a Christian than I had dreamed it could. As I began the Christian adventure, it meant simply confessing a need for God—a kind of recognition that I couldn't handle life alone and that he could help me.

At first, the flood of positive emotions released through the new sense of being loved and understood by God almost overwhelmed me with a sense of joy and well-being. It was like a honeymoon period. For a while reason, and particularly my critical faculties, were temporarily set aside. As in a love relationship between a man and woman, the initial admiration and acceptance blotted out "differences of opinion" between God and me. Such a honeymoon period may be psychologically necessary, as it is in deep human relationships. A bond must be created which will hold through the pain that inevitably follows—if the relationship is going to be deep and lasting.

The way this has happened with me in my relationship with God is something like this. In my inner life, I began to bring Christ into my "rocking-chair room." At first I praised him, thanked him and told him how much I loved him. Feeling his understanding and acceptance of me "just as I was" gave me a great motivation to live for him and to tell other people about him. I had confessed my most basic sin, that of trying to be God in my own world of relationships, and was very relieved since the role of always having to be number one with everyone is a little heavy to carry.

Hiding Our Feelings and Sins

But after a while—I don't remember how long—there came an uneasiness in my inner life. I realized something was wrong in my relationship with God—and also with the people around me. I was spiritually sluggish and started thinking about "my rights" in my relationships. And yet I couldn't see anything I was doing that should cause the misery and sense of alienation from myself which I felt. After all, I had accepted forgiveness for things most people denied even feeling. I realized I must be repressing something—hiding it from myself. I never heard committed Christians talk about this particular hidden problem of repression. I think Carl Rogers was right when he said that if there is internal strain and lack of integration, it always seems to be due to the fact that we are repressing feelings from consciousness.

At the height of my misery I cried out to God, "Show me what is the matter!" That evening we were getting ready to go out to dinner. I was shaving, and as I looked into the mirror I suddenly knew what the trouble was: I had a particular sin of which I was very ashamed and which I had never told anyone. I had sort of acted as if this sin didn't exist when I had prayed or talked to God. Dr. Paul Tournier talks about certain kinds of physical blindness in which the image is formed normally at the back of the eye, but the brain takes no cognizance of it. And this was what I had done with a number of sins in my life. I had known at one level that these things were going on, or had happened in the past. But in my inner relationships to God they had not even come up for consideration. I had unconsciously covered them by confessing sincerely but very generally: "Dear God, forgive me for all my sins, etc." But the awareness that this was a cop-out and a cover-up was a crucial realization which really clobbered my self-image. Because, as Tournier points out, if we stop thinking vaguely and generally about loving "people" and think particularly about *our* wife or husband, *our* parents or children, employer or competitor, *our* best friend or the most attractive people around us, or some specific politician or social rival, then we can see how far we fall short of the absolute love required of us by the gospel—and this can be a blow.

Confessing Specific Sins to God

So in agony I confessed the specific sin which had come to mind as I looked in the mirror while shaving. And although I knew God was already aware of the sin, I experienced a definite sense of release. I realized that *specific* confession is somehow necessary for the one confessing to come back to openness with God. This is confusing to many people. They say, "Why confess to God things he already knows?" But somehow these people have missed something of the strange chemistry of personal relationships which transcends ordinary logic.

For example, let's say that you were to return from a trip a day earlier than you had planned. As you were unlocking your back door, you happened to glance over at your neighbor's house and there in his bedroom you saw your mate in the act of commiting adultery. Now, *you* know that she (or he) has sinned against your relationship and *she* knows it, so there is no need for her to *tell* you in order to give you that *information*. But if she *does not* confess *even though you already know,* is there much hope that you can ever again have a deep and trusting relationship?

So I began to search out and confess the things I had consciously and unconsciously withheld from God. And I began to feel much closer to him. I found it good to check regularly and keep short accounts with him through a daily time of prayer which included specific confession of the sins committed the day before. I also learned the hard way that one can be *overly* introspective to his own detriment and spend *too much* time in self-examination. This is another reason Christian friendships and small groups can help provide a balance between wallowing in one's sins and ignoring them. But *I* still didn't let other people know what was going on inside me.

Moving toward Confession before Another Person

Then (as I described in chapter three) I had a breakthrough in a counseling situation in which I admitted something negative about myself to another person. That started a period of Christian friendships in which the style was to be more open about things like my own doubts, fears, failures, and even hopes. This was very freeing and an amazing relief. When I would express a real feeling to another person or a small group and someone would say "me too" or just nod his head, I felt relief, affirmation, and a sense of sanity or normalcy.

But after a period of several years (which included many ups and downs) there came another bad time of restlessness and of pushing God and people away (especially Christians). I wanted to escape them all—even God. (Maybe *especially* God.) I felt bored and disinterested and was very touchy and hostile at home. It was at this point that I realized that there is a distinction between "openness" with people and God and "confession."

I had become increasingly honest in my Christian communication with individuals, in groups and in public speaking situations. But after a while I noticed a strange thing. It was easy for me to be honest about certain things which were terribly painful for other people to admit. My openness was sometimes contagious. But I had the uneasy feeling that sometimes when people came to me in great agony, their sharing of their most fearful secrets was of a totally different order than my own "confessions" of these same feelings. Then I saw that there were certain other very painful areas in my own life of which I did *not* speak to Christian friends or groups. With a sense of shock I understood what Dag Hammarskjöld meant when he said "Narcissus leant over the spring, enchanted by his own ugliness, which he prided himself upon having the courage to admit." [1]

I was so fascinated at the freedom to be open that I got enchanted with the process and with the fact that I could risk revealing myself. But there were certain things, particularly one sin in my past, with which I was not enchanted. And I was afraid that if I confessed it I would not be acceptable to my Christian friends. I realized even then that the sin wasn't all that "big"—I heard things the world would consider much worse almost weekly. But to me it was intolerable. Because of my pride, I expected myself not to be as weak as other people.

I had heard Bruce and others say that one should find a Christian friend and confess. But I had felt that my deepest sins were for God's ears alone—especially since I was a Protestant. Then I read some of the writings of Luther and Calvin. Luther, far from doing away with confession, said that private confession to a brother "is useful, even necessary, and I would not have it abolished. Indeed I rejoice that it exists in the Church of Christ for it is a cure without equal for distressed consciences. For when we have laid bare our own conscience to our brother and privately made known to him the evil that lurked within, we receive from our brother's lips the word of comfort spoken by God himself. And if we accept this in faith, we find peace in the mercy of God speaking to us through our brother." [2] Calvin also urged the practice of private confession.[3]

Resistance to Confessing before Another Person

But I discovered that at least one reason specific private confession has almost passed from the scene in the Protestant churches is that there are great psychological barriers in the way of true confession. For one who is a minister, Sunday school teacher, community or business leader, or public witness for Christ to face the fact *before another* human being that he has shameful, grubby, and selfish "inexcusable" sins is a real ego insult. So to confess before another person who might tell is really difficult. And, as I have indicated, if confession comes easily it may not be confession in the true sense at all. It may be an ego trip. Authentic confession is always a hard struggle for me.

Tournier has said that there are two stages, two kinds of censorship or resistance involved in the sort of confession which can bring healing: first, one must find enough basic hope or trust in someone or something to overcome the unconscious "censorship" *which keeps our sins repressed from our own consciousness.* And this trust often comes for the Christian through commitment to Christ and Christian friendship of the kind I've been discussing.

The other inner resistance is that which tries to prevent us from confessing the painful memory to another person after it is conscious. But once a person does overcome these resistances and confesses one such threatening memory, then the door is often opened and he may become conscious of many more repressed feelings, sins, and fears. As he recognizes and confesses a previously unacceptable behavior or feeling, the psychic energy which was bound up repressing it is released. And one's sense of strength and field of consciousness are enlarged. This is experienced as an expanded personal freedom and increased awareness of life and relatedness to people and God.

Also one's physical health can improve through confession, since if conflict is not resolved at a conscious level it may be, and often is, expressed in its unsolved form on a more basic or physical level through symptoms like headaches and stomach aches.

Taking the Risk

But notwithstanding all this, it was with a great amount of fear and resistance that I first confessed to God before a Christian friend. I was almost certain he would not respect me any more. But I could not stand myself any longer. It is interesting, now that I think about it, that I picked a man whom I knew who had serious problems in his own life. As Albert Camus said, "We rarely confide in those who are better than we. Rather we are more inclined to flee from their society. Most often, on the other hand, we confess to those who are like us and who share our weaknesses." [4] As I began my first confession, I was tempted to say: "Lord, *if* I have sinned in doing this, forgive me." But when we say, "If I have sinned," to God or people, we take away the essential element of vulnerability which makes forgiveness really cleansing. So I just said to God: "I *have* sinned in this matter. Forgive me."

And miracle of miracles—or so it seemed to me—my friend *did* accept me, and even seemed to feel more close to me as we prayed together and he assured me of God's forgiveness. I was more free at that moment than I had been since I had become a Christian. Later, I read William James's statement and knew it was true: "For him who confesses, shams are over and realities have begun; he has exteriorized his rottenness. If he has not actually got rid of it, he at least no longer smears it over with a hypocritical show of virtue—he lives at least on a basis of veracity." [5]

Later, at another crisis in my life, I went through formal confession in the office of an Episcopal priest, and I found this of great value as he told me in the name of the church of Christ's forgiveness. But the priest was also a man I knew and loved and who had shared deeply with me. There are some ministers to whom I would not want to go for confession.

It is interesting to me that a Roman Catholic who had gone to formal confession all his life told a friend that he himself had missed the confessing and release I am discussing. For it never occurred to him to confess some of the things he had learned about himself through association and prayer with fellow strugglers on the Christian adventure. He had a more or less standardized list of things he had learned to confess, and he too had repressed a bunch of sins.

I don't really know how to say what I am feeling at this point, since I know something about the resistance you may have to confessing before another person. I know that people have very different privacy thresholds. But when something secret is festering within and is really threatening to our self-image, I have a suspicion that almost all of us are afraid of being revealed. And I have no need to tell you that *you* should find someone and confess. I can only say that *I* find specific private confession of great value when done in the presence of a trusted brother or sister—even though I still resist (*especially* if I have to confess a sin I have already confessed once and have "done again"). But when I finally get the courage to go, each time I smile afterwards and remember that confession was never meant to be torture to souls but to set them free. And when I am truly repentant and confess, I realize that I am merely returning to the *full power* and *faith* which I deserted when I sinned. For I am convinced that Christ's promise once made remains forever and that he is always ready to receive us with open arms when we return.

Confession in Groups

Ideally, I believe the fellowship of believers should eventually become open enough that total personal confession could take place either privately with any other member or publicly in the group, as was the case in the early church. But we have drifted so far from the trust and security of such basic honesty, that I am suggesting most groups would do well to begin the process slowly which may lead to a confessional community.

I know that some of you who read this may already be in such a confessional group and think I am overly cautious. But my own experience makes me put in a warning about "instant total honesty" in a church. Because of the great threat to the majority of people and the potential of damage of an unloving or "too easy" honesty, I believe it's good to start slowly. This can be done by creating a small-group atmosphere in which people can begin to express feelings safely and move gently toward deeper, more threatening material.

One rule which has helped some group members from attacking each other with "honesty" is that if anyone brings up a personal problem he must use the *first person singular*. This rule of thumb leads toward a more confessional kind of honesty. And later others can accept criticism and conflict much easier from one they have heard confess.

I realize something of the natural fear in Christian circles, augmented by modern advertising, of being considered weak and inadequate and thus being rejected and despised. But I am encouraged by the belief, expressed so well by a friend, that "God prefers the poor, the weak, the despised. What religious people have much more difficulty in admitting is that He prefers sinners to the righteous. This is explained precisely by the biblical viewpoint and is confirmed by modern psychology; namely, that all men are equally burdened with guilt. Those called righteous are not free from it but have repressed it; those called sinners are aware of it and are, for that reason, ready to receive pardon and grace." [6]

And to people like me who are afraid to confess, this is very good news!

Chapter Five

Communicating "The Faith"

MEMORANDUM

TO: Bruce

FROM: Keith

RE: Chapter Five—Communicating "The Faith"

Dear Bruce:

Now I suppose our problem is to discuss how ordinary people who have admitted they (we) are sinners can communicate a two-thousand-year-old faith in ways which relate to people where they are **now.**

I remember your saying that there are different levels or channels on which "truth" is learned—some more relevant than others. Also, if you have space, how about something on the specific basic need God meets in each Christian life and how that need relates to the particular shape his message to others will take? Other questions which pop into my mind are: How much should you consider where your audience is—that is, what they can grasp? And basically what **is** the Christian message?

Keith

P.S. Frankly, I find it hard to communicate about communicating. Also, it's easier to communicate with strangers who don't know my weaknesses than with members of my family—who do. Would you care to write about that?

What Is "The Message"?

My wife and I were enjoying the pool at our hotel in California. A woman, about forty, came up and took the recliner next to us. As she was arranging her things, I noticed that she had a straw purse with something like a cross-stitch sampler attached to one side. The motto on the sampler said, in bold colored thread, "You can't be too rich or too thin."

I smiled at her and asked, "Do you really believe that?"

"You bet I do!" she answered.

Well, I don't know whether she was too rich, but she obviously was not too thin. However, there was no doubt about her convictions. Her communication was clear. The world knew what she thought life was all about.

All of this made me aware that unknowingly most of us are figuratively wearing a similar sign advertising our deepest convictions about life. I had a fascinating week at a Transactional Analysis Institute taught by Tom and Amy Harris, authors of the book, *I'm OK—You're OK*. During one of the lectures Amy said that a great many adults seem to be wearing an imaginary sweatshirt that says on the front, "How am I doing, Mom?" Across the back are the words, "Try harder!"

Well, this is a clever way of saying that a lot of us give the impression that we are trying to live up to the expectations of a parent (living or dead!) whom we will probably never please.

In the area of communication we have all been affected by Marshall McLuhan's "the medium is the message" philosophy. The things I've been writing over this decade certainly attest to my belief in this emphasis. I've called it relational or incarnational communication. If you have read anything I've written, you have heard me say repeatedly that who you are as a person is as important as what you're saying.

But having said that, I also believe that we Christians have a unique message and that sometimes the message *is* the message. You do not have to be pure and loving, winsome and sincere,

88 / Bruce Larson

with pleasant breath and no body odor to yell, "Fire!" in a burning theater. In a case like that, *the message is the message.*

We Christians have a basic message that in a sense is quite independent of who we are. The words of the Apostles' Creed sum up this basic message for most Christians. In simple terms we believe that God is the Creator of the world; we believe that he took on human form and lived among us in Jesus Christ, who was equally God; we believe he died on the cross and was raised from the dead and that his Spirit is now in us and with us. But all Christians who believe this basic message are not necessarily communicating the same thing to the world.

What Is Your Message—About The Message?

To the universal message that Jesus loves us and died for us and rose again, each of us brings his own imperative. I am speaking of your "therefore" that follows the Apostles' Creed. To find yours, try imagining how you would fill in this sentence if you were teaching a communicants class: "Jesus loves you, and therefore you must _____." What you would put in that blank is probably the message on your imaginary sweatshirt. Is it: "Try harder," "Be good," "Memorize Scripture," "Love God," "Don't be angry," "Tithe," "Witness," "Change the world," "Join the church," "Win souls"?

I am at the place where I seriously question whether the wording on my imaginary sweatshirt has really said what I now believe to be the incredible "good news" of the gospel. I suspect that those who have known me, loved me, and worked closely with me in the past would attribute to me the words, "Try harder." But that is *not* the dominant shape of truth in my life today.

What Is "Truth" Now?

One of the signs of hope that I feel marks the new era ahead is a radical reinterpretation of the basic message and its implications for life together as the people of God. We still have to answer the famous question Pontius Pilate put to Jesus, "What is truth?"

Truth is not always obvious. Jesus says to us as Christians, "I am the way, the truth, and the life." But even knowing and believing that does not entirely solve the question. It seems to me that there are at least four different levels of truth that you and I must deal with.

The first I'll call *timeless truth*. This is the kind of truth which is as eternal as springtime and as reliable as the sunrise. It never gets outmoded or stale. Some of the truth discovered in the world of science is this kind of truth. Certainly the law of gravity can never be superseded. In the spiritual world the law of grace is a similar timeless truth.

Probably the most influential theologian of the twentieth century is Karl Barth. When someone asked him the most profound truth he knew, he said, "Jesus loves me this I know, / For the Bible tells me so." The truth of God's love and the revelation of that truth through the Bible are eternally relevant. If only all truth were in this category, life would be simpler.

However, the question becomes more complicated as we move to the next level of truth which is *timely truth*. Now here we are talking about things that are true, but no longer relevant or fresh. An insight on this came to me one day as I was riding in an airport limousine in New York City. I was catching up on some desperately overdue homework when our bus entered a midtown tunnel. Plunged into blackness and unable to read, I groped overhead and found the switch that turned on the tiny reading light. Instantly a shaft of light lit up the papers in my lap and I could continue my work.

After several minutes the bus emerged into Brooklyn and daylight. The amazing thing is that the shaft of light which had been so important to me in the tunnel was now not only unnecessary but invisible. The ray of light which had been so essential for those three or four minutes was now indiscernible, though the light was still on.

I believe that much of the truth we have received from God in our personal and institutional lives is like that. We receive an insight which is electrifying and illuminating. But in time that truth becomes obscured because of a much greater light. It is still there and it is still true, but it is simply irrelevant and unnecessary at a later time in our lives.

Imagine that two people are suddenly kidnapped and thrown into a dark basement without light. They don't know what dangers might befall them in that basement: spiders, open trap doors, water, or any number of unknown horrors. Suppose, then, that one of those people has a pocket flashlight. With it they can begin to explore their prison and even look for a way out. That light would be the most important thing in the world for those two at that moment. Ultimately, they might discover a light switch, turn it on, and light up the whole basement. The flashlight would immediately become irrelevant.

In looking back over the years, I have discovered several things that were at the time a "new truth," as perhaps you have done. Some of those early discoveries have ushered in a whole new age for me. But as people around me receive more light and move into more new areas, how often I can be left behind, saying, "But what about my flashlight? It saved our lives. Have you forgotten how important it is?"

The dietary laws in the Old Testament made great sense to the people of those times. For example, they were told not to eat pork or shellfish at a time when there was no refrigeration. Those laws surely saved people's lives. Such laws are less relevant for most of us today, though they are still true in places with no refrigeration.

The Reformation centered in the discovery of the centrality of the Bible, a fact so accepted by most Christians today that churches who still make a great point of telling the world that this is their major emphasis are considered conservative and even perhaps reactionary.

In our own time we have seen the witness of the laity emerge as an exciting dimension of Christian communication. But this new strategy will simply open more doors for a ministry by the laity and will be followed by a more complete truth.

Another dimension of truth has become apparent to me more recently and that is *fantasy as truth*. Recently I was at the Menninger Foundation for a week-long seminar. One of their teaching psychiatrists shared an amazing conviction that underlies their sensitive work with people there. "We are convinced," he said, "that fantasy, not reality, will determine what a person does and becomes." In other words, the things you believe to be true may be more important than the facts when it comes to motivating your behavior.

I am aware that I need to understand this basic truth in the area of communicating in relationships. Recently my wife and I were flying home from an exciting conference. As sometimes happens after a spiritual high, we got into a dreadful fight on the plane. We spent the entire trip from California to Baltimore attacking each other and defending ourselves.

All that night and the next day I kept wishing that our conversation on the plane had been bugged. I was convinced that by simply playing the tape of what really happened I could straighten out my relationship with Hazel. She kept quoting things I said that I knew I had never said, while she denied things that I knew I had heard her say. I was sure that only a tape of what really happened would solve the whole problem.

Then I remembered the truth I had learned from the Menninger staff. I realized that Hazel has been programed for twenty-two years to understand me. No tape of what really happened would untangle our relationship. What we thought was said turned out to be far more real than what was actually said. It was only as we were able to listen to each other without defending the "truth" that we could begin to understand the cause of the argument.

If we are to live in love with one another as the Bible enjoins, we must take seriously the fantasies and preconceptions of those with whom we live and work and worship. We must take these fantasies seriously for, in fact, in the relational dimension of Christian communication they supersede truth.

Finally, we are all affected powerfully by *nonverbal truth*. Truth is partly something we can articulate, but it is also something we can communicate nonverbally. Think of the parent who keeps saying, "I love you," but acts out hostility, rejection, or indifference. Psychologists tell us, and we know from our own experience, that what we feel from another person determines the relationship more than what we hear them say. We may hear from the pulpit on Sunday that God loves us, but if church members treat us as though we are not loved, it is very difficult to believe that "truth" from the pulpit.

As an example of nonverbal truth, I remember that when I was a boy growing up we bought a car about every ten years. The first thing we did with the new car was to slipcover the seats. A set of covers would last for several years and when they wore out we would replace them with new slipcovers. At the end of nine or ten years we would trade the car in, usually for junk, with brand-new upholstery. I often wondered who was going to sit on those brand-new seats of our worn-out old car.

As a child, the nonverbal message came to me loud and clear. We Larsons were not good enough to sit on brand-new seats. They were for someone else, not for us. Maybe the junk man would sit on them as he drove the car off to some old automobile graveyard.

Perhaps that illustrates why an incident from my eighth grade class in Evanston, Illinois, made such a profound impression on me. We had all been asked to give a report on "The Most Unusual Person I've Ever Known." One girl said that person was her mother. It seems that the mother served meals to her family every day using the best china and silver. She did this because she believed "There is no one as important to me as my family."

As an eighth grader, that story blew my mind. In my home I used to wonder who the good china and silver were being saved for. Sometimes we had company and it was used, but the nonverbal message I received was that it was too good for us.

It seems to me that nonverbal truth is communicated best by "models." We are told that monkeys who are raised without living mothers do not know how to become mothers. Motherhood is not innate. It is learned from models. As we try to understand what love is and practice it, you and I are surrounded by people who are modeling and communicating nonverbally what love is. In the same way, you and I are models for others. The truth we model will usually be a more effective communication than the truth we tell.

What Need Does Your Message Speak To?

Two recent parables from my own life gave me a new awareness of how I can best communicate truth to other people.

The first parable began when the Larsons moved to Columbia, Maryland. We had been living in New Jersey and I had commuted to Manhattan for twelve years. Now, I miss New York City. I can't pretend I don't. But one of the things I miss the least is the daily commuting which required two trains, four subways, two long walks, and two car rides. This took up three to four hours of each day.

The new city of Columbia was just in the process of being built and much of it is like the pastoral countryside of the last century. There are no subways yet!

Just at the time we moved, a friend of mine, a man about my age, shared with me some advice that his doctor had given him.

Communicating "The Faith" / 93

It seems that to stay alert and keen in the middle years he feels that we all need to have a little danger in our lives. The doctor personally had taken up flying and was convinced that an hour or two a week up in the sky was making him a better doctor, husband, Christian, and, in fact, a better man.

It seemed a wonderful excuse for doing what I had wanted to do for years, and so I bought a motorcycle.

After some shopping around with my fifteen-year-old son, we finally settled on the smallest full-size motorcycle that Honda makes, a Trail 90. This meant that my son could use the motorcycle to ride in the woods around our house and certainly it would be the most economical and adventurous way for me to travel the five miles to and from the office.

Well, it's no small matter getting a motorcycle licensed and registered, not to mention passing the test for your personal license. But the great day finally came and I was ready for my maiden run to the office. Wearing my best business suit and tie and with my briefcase strapped on behind the small but efficient machine, I started out.

Since about one-fourth mile of the journey entailed traveling on a four-lane super highway, I picked a late morning hour so that I would not get into heavy traffic. All went well and by the time I reached the highway I was moving along at a speedy thirty-five mph. Suddenly, coming at me in the opposite direction at about seventy mph was what motorcyclists refer to as the "ultimate machine." It was a huge Honda 750 carrying a burly young cyclist with his chick hanging on behind, both in black leather jackets, long hair flowing out from under each helmet.

Well, as we were about to pass each other, the driver raised his left arm in the "ride on" salute that motorcyclists give. I cautiously looked around to see who was following me and discovered that mine was the only vehicle on the road. Obviously he meant me! I had been accepted into that great fellowship of "easy riders" my first time out!

Timidly, I gave him back a "ride on" as he whisked by. I could not believe that getting into this mysterious fraternity would be so easy. Simply by spending several hundred dollars for a tiny machine, with no credentials, no experience, and not even the proper uniform, I was one of them. No questions asked!

I returned home from the office that night looking for motorcycles. Spotting one a great way off, before he could even see me clearly, I greeted him with the "ride on" sign which he loyally returned. Since then, whenever I ride, I find our special fellowship quick to greet one another.

Now to understand what this means to me you have to understand one of the basic anxieties of my life. I have a deep-seated fear of being the odd man out—the one who doesn't fit—the one who is inappropriate for the occasion. I have recurring nightmares of being at a party without my trousers on, or being in the pulpit without a single note or idea, or taking an examination for which I have not studied.

If the gospel is to be good news for people like me, it has to say, "Welcome, you are one of us; you're home free; come on in —you belong to us; we belong to you." Well, in a small way on my little motorcycle this is exactly what happened and keeps happening. An exciting group of people have found me acceptable and have *included* me. And that is the basic conscious need the gospel message continually meets in *my* life.

So it seems to me this is exactly the kind of message that the church must communicate to the world and to the non-Christian.

All too often in a strange Christian group I feel I am being measured to see if I have the right theology, the right experience, or the right ethic. I am being judged by whether I am as loving as they are, as prophetic, as involved, as sacrificial, or as pure.

To me the mark of the Christian is that he is one who believes he is loved by God apart from his credentials and performance. If we are so loved simply by the grace of God in Jesus Christ, then we must communicate to the other person that he is so loved. He is one of us because he is one of "the loved"!

What Can Your Audience Understand?

Now the second parable occurred some months later on a hot, spring day. I was driving that same motorcycle across a more rural part of my route near a great swamp, when I suddenly had to swerve to avoid hitting a box turtle sitting in the middle of the road. Eager to be a St. Francis and save the life of my hard-shell friend, I stopped and went back to pick him up and move him off the road. But in the midst of my good deed for the day I changed my mind. I decided instead to play a trick on him. I put him in my pocket and brought him to the office. All day long he was the center of attention. Beautiful secretaries, busy executives, and as-

Communicating "The Faith" / 95

sorted visitors all fussed over him. He sat in air-conditioned splendor eating bacon, bread, peanut butter, lettuce, and whatever his little heart desired.

The staff ate lunch together at the office and on this particular day a friend joined us and brought her guitar. So along with everything else he heard beautiful music, great singing, and all the while continued to stuff his belly full of exotic foods.

That night at five o'clock I brought him back to the same place in the road where I found him, carried him to the side, and headed him toward the swamp. And then it hit me. I wondered what kind of a tale he would tell his friends. How could he communicate to them the wonders of air-conditioning; the topography and geography of an office building; the experience of being surrounded by beautiful girls, of eating strange foods, and of hearing wonderful music and singing? I'm sure that from that time forward he became known as "Crazy Charlie" to all the other turtles in the swamp. There is no way that experience can ever be communicated to his friends. The more he tries, the more alienated and estranged he will become.

Crazy Charlie is like many Christians who have had a dramatic conversion or a mountaintop experience of ecstasy. They try to relate what happened to people who have no experiential reference for understanding them, and often they simply alienate others and minimize their own credibility.

Blaise Pascal, the brilliant French mathematician, scientist, inventor, and mystic, was one of the great saints of all time. In his room late one night he had the experience of seeing a fire burning and hearing God speak to him out of that fire. But no one ever knew about this transforming experience in Pascal's life until after his death, when a written record was found sewn in the lining of his coat. Apparently, whenever he doubted God, he could feel the paper in his coat and know and remember that special time of God's communication with him. He must have realized that to share that mystical moment with people would be of no avail. That is *not* how you help people. Instead, his ministry centered in inventing labor-saving devices and in writing two beautiful books of theology and inspiration. The esoteric experience that changed his life was something personal between God and himself. He knew that in trying to communicate the good news, you start where your audience is, not where you are.

And that's what I think God is up to. He begins with us where we are in the events of our daily lives to teach us what it means to live with him the Great Adventure, and to communicate the gospel to others he tells us to "go and do likewise."

MEMORANDUM

TO: Keith

FROM: Bruce

RE: Chapter Five—Communicating "The Faith"

Dear Keith:

I tried to deal with the questions you mentioned. But in looking over my part of this chapter (which is enclosed) I realize that I didn't give any specific guidelines or suggestions about how one person might become involved with another and talk to him specifically about becoming a Christian.

I remember your discussing with me the problems of sharing the gospel years ago. I think it would be great if you could take us through the process of communicating your faith the way you did for me.

Bruce

Are Words Necessary?

As I began to be serious about living the Christian adventure, I tried to discover a way to articulate something of the reality I was finding in my own experience. I realized almost immediately that "saying words" is not what is meant by communicating the reality of Jesus Christ. I think this is true regardless of how theologically correct the words may be.

In my reaction against legalistic, verbal, religious "scalp gathering," I had for years decided that I would live my faith instead of talk about it. Now I saw how selfish this "live the faith and not talk about it" idea is. It reminds me of a man in a dread disease ward marvelously meeting the doctor who had perfected a cure. The patient, as he was being (secretly) cured, walked back and forth in the same ward sort of flexing his muscles as he moved beds around and variously helped the other patients die more comfortably. His display of new wholeness only led the other patients to envy him . . . leaving their own deep illness unattended to. I saw that this patient had somehow to introduce his dying fellows to the physician so that they too could begin to be healed from their loneliness and incompleteness. I realized that I was this patient. This introduction to Christ, I saw, would take some *words* of direction or at least indication.

As I began to ask outstanding church leaders how one person might tell another about the realness of God, I found that this business of effectively communicating Christian reality, of "witnessing," is probably one of the least understood areas of Christian living today, particularly among educated people. Everyone I talked with beat around the bush. They simply did not know how to do this without being pious or obscure. I decided to try to see for myself what true effectiveness in sharing the Christian message and life might include. Immediately I was stumped.

What Is Effective?

Who can properly judge his own true effectiveness in other

people's lives? I can remember a particularly cold and snowy winter night in Indiana. It was after supper. The wind was howling outside and we felt very cozy. Mary Allen was doing some sewing in one corner, and I was trying to read the newspaper on the sofa across the room. Our three little girls were giggling and climbing all over me as if I were a ladder. Finally I stopped trying to read and began to wrestle with them and love them. Through the tangle of little arms and legs I happened to see Mary Allen across the room . . . with tears of happiness streaming down her face.

Being Ourselves. I began to see that I, and the people I know, are most winsome in our intimate relationships when we are unconsciously being ourselves with other people and accepting them just as they are, without trying to manipulate or change them in any way. But the very lack of self-consciousness that is so attractive makes those things we do at such times difficult to analyze.

A minister often thinks he is most effective for God in the pulpit on that Sunday morning when he is preaching an eloquent sermon after hours of preparation. But between the nine and eleven o'clock services when he is in the process of going from one service to another—trying to relax a moment—someone urgently grabs his arm and says, "The superintendent of the children's department didn't come this morning!" So the minister has to go into the children's chapel and speak. He goes in and shares informally something of himself or the gospel message, never knowing as he rushes out to the next service that the mind of a little visitor on the back row was struck by his impromptu words—and offered himself to God. Perhaps a great Christian life has been conceived —and the minister never knows.

Sharing Consciously. I think a great deal of what happens deeply and positively to other people through our lives happens in this way. But, on the other hand, I found that there are a great many things we can learn consciously about sharing the newness of the Christian life and message. Most committed Christians have a great deal they could say about the reality and love of God, the relief of forgiveness, and the gift of purpose and relatedness to a life once filled with confusion and lack of meaning. Most of us have some things we might share in our business and social lives if only we knew how to go about it with real perception in the language we use for everyday living, so that we won't be hypocritical. The new groups of lay disciples in America are finding that one can sometimes get this message of salvation and a new life across. And I want to discuss here specifically one way this can be done, or attempted, in the lives of people like many of us in the church today.

Two Levels of Communicating a Living Faith

I think there are at least two levels of communicating living Christianity; and most of the people with whom I had been acquainted knew only about the first level. For the great majority of church-going people, effective sharing of Christianity consists of studying the Bible and related books, speaking to lay groups about God, Sunday school teaching, preaching, living the Christian ethical life, being a good churchman, husband, and businessman, having an active concern for the important social and political issues of our time, and helping the poor. Most of us think a man who does all these things (layman or minister) is really getting God's message across. Often such a person develops quite a reputation as a speaker and Christian leader. But as important as this level of Christian sharing is, I have become convinced that it is only "contact work" for the Lord; and for years we have made it the whole enterprise. This type of Christian living and speaking often spreads a warm religious aura in a group; but it leaves few deeply and permanently changed lives in its wake. And without deeply changed and growing lives, there can be no renewed church, no changed world, regardless of how full the churches are.

The second level of Christian sharing is that which is being reborn in the life of the church today. It is a person-to-person ministry, an actual conscious readiness on the part of an individual Christian to put another man or woman in touch with the living God. This is not another "pat system" or "semi-canned sales pitch." It is rather a way of thinking about and being related to other people. It is an attitude based on the realization that, behind the remarkably placid masks of the faces we see every day on the streets and in our businesses and clubs, there lies a world of twisting souls, living with frustration and the fear of failure and meaninglessness, a world of souls without rudders, without any real sense of ultimate direction.

The Hunger for God—Behind the Mask

I think we in America may be the "masters of deceit" in our

personal lives. We have even deceived ourselves. We wear masks of success and happiness and integrity so much that we have even convinced ourselves that we are not such a bad people. Consequently we have not the basic prerequisite for coming to God—a conscious sense of sin or separation from him. Or at least so it would appear. Modern writers have made much of the lack of man's sense of sin today. Some years ago Reinhold Niebuhr spoke of "the universality of this easy conscience among moderns." [1] Although I think this generalization is far too broad, I do know that many people in our generation do not sense their basic separation from God (or sin) as guilt. Today this separation often manifests itself in our vague indefinable restlessness, incompleteness, and loneliness, often culminating in an awful sense of meaningless depersonalization. So if one goes about trying to capitalize on men's conscious guilt to get them into a personal relation with God, he may miss many of the sharpest people altogether and drive them away from Christ, since they simply don't experience their basic problem as guilt.

I have spoken to dozens of groups of all sizes and hundreds of individuals these past years; and I have never faced a group in which I was not convinced that many of the people were crying out in the privacy of their own hearts for some peace and direction in their souls. What I am saying is that there is a very *real need* for the life and message Christ brings; and this need is not far beneath the surface of modern life. This needs to be said since so many people are discouraged about sharing the Christian life when people look so self-sufficient all around them.

A Look at One Approach

This is the way this kind of sharing might work. First, you find yourself in contact with another person, a natural, normal contact. Right here I think many Christians get off the track. I am so egotistical that when I became a Christian I was sure that I was sent to witness to the most outstanding group I knew (whom I considered my peers). But in reading the New Testament I was somewhat stunned to realize that even Jesus Christ evidently never made it in his hometown, with his own local peer group (Mark 6:1 f.). And this did not seem to disturb or deter him in the least.

So I began to look around me at all the people whom God had already put in my life with whom I might develop a deeper and more personal relationship. I realized that, without changing my daily routine one bit, I had a world filled with people, most of whom I had been ignoring for years. There was the man who sometimes helped me in the yard. There were the fellows in the gas station I traded with all the time, the parking lot attendants, the service people in the office building, the waiters at the Petroleum Club, the secretaries, the bank tellers, and other men with whom I had coffee occasionally—and my own wife and children. As I began to see these as important people who need God and his love, I realized that many of us active American churchmen are stumbling over the bodies of our wives and children and people in our daily paths in order to participate in time-consuming, promoted evangelistic programs.

As I began to read the New Testament accounts, I saw that Christ almost never "went out of his way" to help anyone. He seems to have walked along and helped the people in his path. He was totally focused on doing God's will and going where God led him. But he never failed to help the people he met along the way while going where God directed him. This made for an amazing steadiness and spiritual economy in his direction and ministry. This one change in my perspective made witnessing not a program but part of *a way of life*.

Free but Not Cheap—a Matter of Attitude

The second thing I realized was that we Christians have so cheapened the Christian message that most thinking people don't want any part of it. Our attitude betrays our lack of real faith. We act as if we were selling tickets to something, or memberships, instead of introducing people to Almighty God in an eternal and conscious relationship. When a person buys a theater ticket he doesn't even have to think about it, and his attitude and verbal exchange with the ticket girl reflect this. But when you walk into a room in which two large corporations are about to consummate a merger, there is an air of gravity. Even a casual observer can tell that something important is taking place—because of the attitudes of the participants as they go about their business.

I think non-Christians do not read this kind of importance into our attitude when we are talking to them about Christianity. So I would say that in this kind of witnessing, we must think and pray in terms of a much larger God, a much greater and more transforming gift of life. I came to see that if people do not really believe we have found something that is terribly important to us, why should they want it?

The Inner Encounter

After an outward personal contact has been made, then the real contact is made with the person behind the mask. I have found that this is done mostly by listening with real interest. As I've indicated earlier, I believe that what you are doing when you are listening as a Christian is putting your hand quietly in the other person's life and feeling gently along the rim of his soul until you come to a crack—some frustration, some problem or anguish you sense that he may or may not be totally conscious of. The magic of this kind of concern is that you will often find your conversation moving imperceptibly from the general surface talk of the world situation and the weather into the intimate world of families and of hopes, of his life and yours.

And when one begins to listen honestly to people for Christ's sake, with a word or look of encouragement, they often begin to cast out before you the shadows of a great number of the fears and uncertainties which are crouching just inside their hearts. Of course this account is greatly oversimplified for some relationships, but not for many (if you are really interested in the person).

In approaching life this way, do not think of the person you are listening to as a prospect for the church or as an object for your Christian witness. I know this may sound strange, but thinking in these terms produces a kind of spiritual manipulation. And instead of really listening you will be saying to yourself, "How can I get this conversation around to *spiritual* things?" Besides, from the other person's perspective your anxiety to get your "Christian content" across sends out the unspoken message that you have something more important on your mind (he doesn't know what it is) than him and what he has to say.

So I began merely to listen to people with the idea in mind of making friends for Christ. Soon I found that I could identify with almost every problem or sin I heard—if not with the deed, certainly with the emotion behind it. And this honest identification freed some people to be their real selves. It became a bridge across which we could walk into each other's lives. I found my life filled with a new and deeper kind of friendship than I had ever known before. But the point is that this kind of sharing begins not by spouting your *answer,* but rather by finding out who this person is and his problem, his need—*as he sees it.*

In the Gospels I do not see Christ rushing up to people, grabbing them by the arm, and confronting them with a theological question. He seems to have walked down the road and listened to people describe their problems as they saw them. The people seemed to be so surprised and thrilled that someone saw their problems and took them seriously, that I rather imagine many responded totally and were made whole. And yet Christ knew these men's basic human problem was not withered hands or leprosy. But he met them where they were.

Your Own Experience

If and when your friendship with someone grows (and it so often will if you love him), and he acknowledges sometime that his life is not complete, *then* very naturally and simply you may want to tell him how you came to a realization in your own life that it wasn't what it should be and how that realization caused you to turn to God. Tell your friend what God did, not to make you good (Christ was pretty clear about his attitude toward men claiming goodness—see Mark 10:18) but to make you basically more hopeful and joyful. And if you are not basically more hopeful and joyful regardless of the many new problems you have as a Christian, then you had better take a close look at your own relationship with Christ. You may have missed something very important in the gospel yourself.

When you have reached this point, you will know whether or not this person is coolly detached or obviously seeking something in his own life. You know this because you have listened to him over a period of time and know his real interests and needs. But if after hearing about your life, he says something like, "Yes, uh . . . uh . . . say, did you hear what the Yankees did yesterday?" don't panic, feel rejected, and say urgently, "What did I say to offend you?" or, "Don't you understand, friend, I'm about to lead you to salvation?" But rather you might say something more like, "No, what did the Yankees do?" and listen to him. He may only be backing off because you are getting too close to him.

People are spiritually like fawns, ready to dart away at the first sign of what they consider any invasion of privacy. And since you

Communicating "The Faith" / 105

are not selling anything, you do not have to be anxious. We Christians are the only people around who claim to have an eternal life; and yet in our urgency to convince people, we reflect nothing but anxiety and tenseness. But if this person has listened to your telling something about your own life and relationship to God and is interested, then you may be able to help him to see where he is now with regard to the gift of new life God is waiting to give him.

What Is Most Important to You?

This is one way you can help find out where he is in his relationship to Christ. Get him to look inside his own life, honestly. He doesn't have to tell you what he sees (this allows him to keep his privacy while considering what you are saying). Ask him to be specific with himself and with God. Let's say, so that you can see how it might feel to be talked to like this, that you and I are sitting across a luncheon table in a quiet place. We have known each other for some months and have come to the place in our relationship which I have just described. You have been going to church for years, but you are not experiencing the kind of newness in your adult Christian life which we have been discussing. You are really interested in knowing how you might make a new beginning in your own life. I will talk to you here as I would if we were together in the same room. If you are interested, then do the things I will ask you to do.

The first thing I would like for you to do is to look into your own inner life and ask yourself the question, "What is the most important thing in the world to me?" The temptation is to say, "God," but let me tell you how you can tell what is really most important to you. What do you think about again and again when your mind is not engaged with work or with someone else? Here are some suggestions of the kinds of things I mean: Do you think about your wife or husband (or children)? Or the fact that you have none? Do you think about being great in your vocation? Or being considered a brilliant person? Or socially sophisticated? Or are your recurring thoughts about sex or your own beauty? Or are your thoughts when alone centered in your own problems, jealousy, etc.—centered in yourself?

When I ask myself this, some of the things I have come up with at various times in my life (if I am honest) are: Thinking about myself as a successful athlete, businessman, scholar, or writer. Or fantasizing sexual conquests. Or imagining or hoping people will think I am an extremely intelligent person. Or at one time my thoughts were occupied with how I could become a great Christian minister.

Now each of these thoughts is like a rubber ball on a string tied to the center of your mind. You throw it out and get busy with the work of the day. But when you are alone, back it comes again and again to sit in the middle of the stage of your attention. I am asking you to consider this because whatever you focus this hottest intensity of your mind on is very likely *what you worship instead of Jesus Christ!* For what is worship if it is not the object of your life's most intense focus?

I am not implying that Christ says it is wrong to love one's children or wife or vocation. But it is wrong to love them more than God. It is wrong to make idols of them. It ruins them and us. I believe that Christ intimates that we can never fully realize the gift of life which he came to bring us until we first know that we have loved ourselves and our way more than him and his way (see Matt. 9:10–13; Luke 15; 18:18–30).

I have become convinced that the things which keep us from a live relationship to Christ are often not the "bad" things in our lives but the good things which capture our imaginations and keep them from focusing on Jesus Christ. I think this accounts for a good bit of our frustration as church members. We look around in our lives and say, "No stealing, no murder, no adultery! Why, God, am I so miserable and frustrated in my Christian life?" But we have not seen the fact that we have never really offered him the one thing he requires—our primary love.

What does one do when he finds out that he loves something more than God? For me it was rather terrifying, because the thing which was keeping me from the freedom of Christ was my desire to be a great lay minister! Because one's decisions will ultimately be made to conform with the shape of whatever has truly captured his imagination, my own decisions and sacrifices were not being made purely to love and feed Christ's sheep out of obedience and love of him; but rather my decisions were made to help "the church's work" (*my* work) to its greatest fulfillment. This led to chaos and frustration.

When one sees, and can honestly face the fact, that his world is really centered in something besides God—in one's self in fact—I think he faces the most profound crossroads in his life (whether he is a layman or a bishop). Because this is to recognize that one has separated himself from God by taking God's place in the center of his own little world.

Making a Commitment

What does a person do? The answer is paradoxically the simplest and yet the most difficult thing I have ever done. In our age of complexity we want a complex answer, but Christ gives us instead a terribly difficult one. I think there are basically two things involved in coming to God at the center of one's life: (1) To tell God that we do not love him most, and confess specifically what it is that we cannot give up to him. (2) To ask God in the personality of Jesus Christ to come into our conscious lives through his Spirit and show us how to live our lives for him and his purposes —one day at a time.*

But what if you recognize that you honestly do not want God more than whatever is first in your life? I think this is where a good many perceptive Christians find themselves. In that case I would recommend that you (1) confess (as above) and then (2) tell Christ that your honest condition is that you cannot even want him most. But tell him that you want to want him most (if you do), ask him to come into your life at a deeper level than you have ever let him before, and give him permission to win you totally to himself. This may be your first honest encounter with Christ, and he will take you wherever you are. As a matter of fact, I believe this is really all any of us can do—give God per-

---

*I am aware of the arguments of Buber and others against the position that once a man recognizes his idol as such, he can immediately turn the same kind of love on God. The Buber position points out (correctly, I think) that the love of idols is a possessive love, and that if we turn this same kind of love on God, we will blaspheme. "He who has been converted by this substitution of object now 'holds' a phantom that he calls God. But God, the eternal Presence, does not permit Himself to be held. Woe to the man so possessed that he thinks he possesses God" (*I and Thou* [New York: Scribner's, 1970], p. 106).

Since I believe that kind of substitution of one's possessive love has led many evangelical Christians into a state of frustrated misery, I have here been careful to explain that the change I am referring to is from the possessive love of an idol to the responding love which is directed to the One we want to possess us, to guide us, to confront us at the core of our being with his Lordship and Life.

mission to make us his. We certainly cannot be his by our own strength of will.

Some New Perspectives for a New Life

And if you made this new conscious beginning in a conversation with me, this is what I would tell you: that from now on you are not responsible to exert the pressure, the burden of muscling yourself up to be "righteous." You are not promising to change, or to have strength, or to be a great Christian. You have only confessed your need and turned your life over to Christ. What a relief! If he wants me to change, he will furnish the motivating power by giving me the desire to change, and then the strength to do it.*

But how does one begin living this new life every day? If a man makes this sort of new beginning in your presence, don't clap him on the back and walk off whistling. It is a terrifying experience to decide suddenly to give God your will, only to realize that you don't know what to do next. Christianity is not a status at which one arrives; it is a life in which one matures. So show him the first steps one begins to take in this life with God.

Show him how to take a few minutes a day, each day, to begin developing this new relationship. Tell him how to begin reading the Bible every day, and to begin to live and move into it. Tell him to look for the personality of God in all that he does and sees. Show him how to get started at once in a vital sharing life with other strugglers. Take him into your own group and admit you are a struggler too. And if you don't have such a group in your own church, look for one or start one for your own sake. Explain to this person the discouragements that will come in actually trying to live your life for God; describe the doubts; and point beyond them to the joys. Be honest, because there are doubts and discouragements; and unless he knows that you have them, he may doubt his own faith as they hit him when he is all alone.

This kind of sharing of the Christian life and gospel produces more than attenders at church (though it almost always does

---

* This is not advising Christians to sit back and do nothing. It is rather a statement of the paradoxical fact that although good works are inevitable in the deeply committed Christian's life, I do not believe they are required to establish or maintain one's redeemed relationship. The relationship and the strength to live the life are gifts of grace.

Communicating "The Faith" / 109

produce these). For people who have seen themselves and accepted Christ as Lord and Master of their practical lives have not crossed the finish line of the Christian life. For the first time they have climbed down out of the grandstand and gotten on the starting block as participants in that life in the living Body of Christ.

So, as the first level of sharing Christianity is talking on Christian subjects, church school teaching, and Christian living, this second person-to-person level is the far more demanding business of living life, consciously loving person after person, listening to each one personally and privately, and then walking a few steps with him toward the cross, and perhaps putting his hand quietly into the waiting hand of Christ—and his church.

Chapter Six

Money and Possessions

MEMORANDUM

TO: Bruce

FROM: Keith

RE: Chapter Six—Money and Possessions

Dear Bruce:

Talk about "hidden problems," the only advice I got about money as a new Christian was "Tithe"! But the man who told me that made about ten times more than I did at the time and had always had plenty of money.

How about writing something concerning how our backgrounds may affect our attitudes about money? How does the church look at money? What are some of the various attitudes among Christians concerning possessions? And what do **you** think the basic issue is for a Christian who wants to be God's person regarding the use of his money and possessions?

Keith

P.S. Do you think Word will give us a royalty advance on this book?

Background and Money

It saddens me that my three children are weary and bored whenever I talk about "the great days" when we were all poor. To go through a national crisis such as the depression of the 1930s when money and possessions were in short supply for the majority of people, leaves scars. Two friends of mine were also born during that time. Like me, they grew up in middle-class poverty which perhaps was almost worse than being on relief (or so it seemed to me). We were not quite poor enough to get any help, but all around us we saw furniture and cars being repossessed and mortgages being foreclosed.

One of my companions from these not so good old days has grown up with an ever-expanding taste for high living. Nothing is too good for him or his family. He wears the best clothes, always orders à la carte in a restaurant, and drives the latest and most expensive cars. I am convinced that this is the way in which he assures himself he is no longer that little boy leading a meager and deprived style of life.

My other friend seldom buys anything new, but when he does it has usually been on sale and marked down. He consistently lives beneath his means and has a passion for saving. Personally I think that this is his way of reacting to the experience of poverty common to the three of us. Fearful of being poor again, he is guarding against that day when the economic walls may tumble in. (You can appreciate that I am the only one of the three who came through with a healthy attitude about money!)

While almost everyone of my generation is marked by the depression, the children of the fifties and the sixties are marked by their experience of affluence. Many young people who have had a plethora of clothes, stereos, cars, and travel are now hiding in the woods, weaving their own clothes, and eating vegetables from their organic gardens. The abundance or scarcity of money in our childhood is bound to leave marks. Some of us feel guilt about the money we have or the money we wish we had. Contrary to the misquote we hear so often, however, the Bible does not say that money is evil. More accurately, the tenth verse of the sixth chapter of First Timothy says, "The *love* of money is the root of all evil." To me, this means that people of staggering wealth can wear riches like a light-fitting garment which doesn't impede them in life, service, or authenticity. Other people can wear poverty like a suit of armor. This love of money which the author of First Timothy speaks of encumbers them. They are jealous and resentful about relatives or friends or neighbors who are making bigger salaries or who have more possessions. So the problem does not always lie in what we have, but in what we wish we had or feel we ought to have.

The Church's View of Money and Poverty

There are churches who have built whole theologies and systems of life around money. The Protestant church in its beginning years in Europe and America has been credited with the work-hard-live-simply-save-your-money ethic. The clergy of the Roman Catholic church espouse poverty and abstain from the accumulation of things. The Mormons practice a material collectivism much like that of the early church. That popular black preacher, Brother Ike, says that if you really love God and serve him you will be just as rich as Brother Ike. These are just a few examples of how the churches have influenced people's attitudes toward money.

Someone has said that Christianity is the most materialistic religion in the world. We believe in a Jesus who promised not only life everlasting but that some form of physical body will continue past the grave. His own resurrection from the dead was a demonstration of that promise. We deduce from the biblical accounts of his ministry that our Lord was a materialist. He spoke more about feeding the poor and the hungry and caring for the sick and the lepers than he did about meditating and reading the Scriptures. He emphasized using the things of this world as an extension and a demonstration of our faith.

Voluntary poverty is generally considered a noble and admirable way of life. Certain branches of the church have advocated this way of life in one form or another for a long time as a way to seek more unselfish goals. But it is possible to give up riches or material blessings sometimes for the purpose of seeking things even more potent than wealth in the world's sought-after commodities. Robert

Money and Possessions / 115

Louis Stevenson once said, "To have what we want is riches; but to be able to do without is power." In one sense this was the secret of Mahatma Gandhi's whole life. Just before he died, Gandhi was visited by the writer Vincent Sheean. During this visit Gandhi read his own translation of the first verse of a great ancient scripture of India, the Isha Upanishad: "The whole world is the garment of the Lord. Renounce it, then, and receive it back again as the gift of God." This verse seems to account for Gandhi's strategy and political effectiveness.

Recently I was lovingly rebuked by a friend who is a priest for accepting royalties on books about God and Jesus. He also is an author but all of his royalties go to his Order. Beyond that, he reminded me that he was allowed to buy just one new suit every five years and could own nothing and have nothing.

As we pursued this discussion of "practical theology," I reminded him that accepting a vow of poverty for the church is not the only means of living by faith. (Far be it from me to be defensive!) For example, I have the responsibility to provide for my wife and care for and educate my three children. While it was true he owned nothing, he was responsible for no one—not even himself. He is currently housed splendidly, enjoys the best food, and has a guarantee that he will be buried decently and in order at no expense to himself or his family.

Let me add quickly that I know there are thousands of priests and nuns who do live in this country and on the mission field in very humble circumstances, and Protestant missionaries as well. But it seems to me that vows of poverty are not the only way and possibly not even the best way for a Christian to settle this whole matter of his relationship to money and possessions. I happen to believe that a vow of poverty taken in the context of an affluent church is very different from a vow of poverty taken in a situation where no one but God is supporting you.

Romanticizing Poverty and Wealth

I'm constantly surprised at the number of people I talk to who have a very romantic view of poverty in the world. I once met a man sitting by the pool of a luxurious hotel in Switzerland. While I was trying to catch up on some mail, he was ordering lunch, and we began talking. The man had made an enormous amount of money about twenty years ago in the United States and had chosen to come with his third wife to Switzerland to live on that money. He was now enjoying the fruits of his earlier labors. I was and am enough of a believer in free enterprise to accept that. But then he began to talk about what a burden it is to be rich and that really only the poor are happy in this world. He went on to suggest that the poverty which exists in the world because of the indifference of people of affluence like him, and to some degree like myself, is really a blessing to people. I could hardly believe that he was really saying these things.

On the other hand, some of us romanticize money as well. Money is not the solution for all of our problems, but money is power and like all power it can be used for good or evil. I remember hearing once that money is really another pair of feet to walk where Christ would walk, money is another pair of hands to heal and feed and bless the desperate families of the earth. In other words, money is my other self. Money can go where I do not have time to go, where I do not have the skill to go, where I do not have youth to go, where I do not have a passport to go. My money can go in my place and heal and bless and feed and help. A man's money is an extension of himself.

The True Romance of Money

The true drama of money is that I have traded a part of my life for it. I have given my time, my energy, my skill, my wisdom, my training, my gifts to people who have in turn purchased this part of me. In terms of my allotted time I am enfeebled, I am weakened, I am diminished in some sense every time I earn money. So my money is in a real way my very life.

I am also free to assume that the money I have earned is now mine. I can hoard it or use it for illicit or unscrupulous purposes or lend it at exorbitant rates. But if I take that for which I have traded my life and share it with others, I am, in a tangible way, laying down my life for others as Jesus commanded.

The Basic Issue: Stewardship or Ownership?

The basic issue for the Christian, it seems to me, is whether we believe we are stewards or owners of what we possess. A good steward receives gratefully anything his Lord gives to him. But he must account for it and use it wisely. We Christians also believe that this is God's world. Each person is alive by an act of God's loving grace. If material blessings come to us, we believe they are gifts of God for which we are to be responsible as stewards. The whole earth is really ours as stewards.

Now this is a fact which non-Christians may not understand. Most of the world believes in ownership. Whether we believe all should have the same amount of goods and money or whether we should have varying piles in our storehouses—capitalists and socialists alike believe in ownership. We can only challenge people who have this premise to be generous with what they own rather than stingy—responsible rather than irresponsible.

But for the person who believes in God, stewardship is the key. Neither poverty nor riches is the issue. The Apostle Paul said, "I have learned to be satisfied whether I have nothing or whether I have everything." The issue is not really how much you have, but whether or not you are using it as a steward of God.

My wife and I were watching a panel discussion on TV one night. Four women were discussing marriage and the sex relationship. Three of them were advocating free love, while the fourth, the wife of a prominent Christian pastor, was insisting that sex be confined to the marriage bed and that premarital and extramarital sex were categorically wrong. The first three women were articulate, and militant, and this lovely Christian wife and mother obviously lost the argument. After the show, we realized there was no rational way she could defend her position against these clever opponents. Christians operate in the area of sex from a very different code. You cannot justify chastity and the sanctity of marriage apart from a belief in God and a commitment to him. We live this way because we are obedient and because we trust him. If you have no such commitment, chastity does not seem to make much sense.

The same idea applies to money. We Christians operate from a different principle. We believe in stewardship. We do not equate the Kingdom of God with either capitalism or socialism, nor do we say that the Christian stance is either to live in poverty or affluence. Rather it is to be willing to use all that we have for others.

I'm hopeful that there is a way that we can present this idea to the world. The whole notion of stewardship might make sense even to people who do not believe in God. I remember Bishop Edwin Holt Hughes telling about being entertained by a wealthy landowner. He had preached in his host's church that morning on

God's ownership. Looking over his broad acres and remembering the morning sermon, the man asked, "Do you mean to tell me, Bishop, that this land does not belong to me?" The bishop said the answer came to him in a flash, "Ask me that one hundred years from now."

How does one own that which one does not take with him beyond this life? If you have some great old trees on property you own, do you really own them, if they are too big to transplant and you do not choose to cut them down for firewood? You are simply a custodian of something you can enjoy during your lifetime. They will surely be passed on to others along with the hills, the valleys, and the rivers on your property unless you destroy them. To believe we are stewards rather than owners makes great sense to me.

Micro Ethics or Macro Ethics in the World?

Finally, another basic question for Christians who are grappling with the use of money and things in a time of growing world poverty and depression has to do with where you give your money and why. Why do you give to one cause and not another? Why do you save and not give? Why do you buy and not sell, or sell and not buy? Perhaps this is where we need help from many younger Christians today who have rebelled against the Christian establishment and accuse us of being overfocused on micro ethics and minimizing the importance of macro ethics.

Micro ethics are little ethics—those with which we Christians have been preoccupied: smoking, drinking, gambling, playing cards, swearing, conducting business on Sunday, etc. Micro ethics are important inasmuch as they make up our practical day-to-day Christianity. But young radical Christians today demand that we be concerned with macro ethics as well. These have to do with injustice, poverty, hunger, civil liberty, and equal opportunity. Macro ethics affect the lives of great numbers of people.

For example, in the past a person may have chosen not to use alcohol simply to keep his own body healthier and his mind clear. These are micro ethics and they are valid. But an example of the macro ethic in regard to alcohol is simply that the amount of grain used to produce one quart of alcohol could feed many people for several days. The consumption of alcohol has formerly been a micro ethical decision. Today it is also a macro ethical decision.

The president exhorts us to clean our plates and eat less. Senators advocate skipping a meal once a week. All of this falls somewhere between micro and macro ethics. But our national farm program for years has been programed to feed grain to cattle because we have been embarrassed in the past by our huge grain surpluses. There is probably no more wasteful use of grain in terms of food than to feed it to cattle who are in turn slaughtered for food. Not only that, there are many famine-ridden nations in the world who export more protein and food to the United States than they import or receive from us. We buy the entire peanut crop from some of Africa's poorer nations in order to feed our cattle. We then send them a token amount of grain. And of course our meat consumption as a nation, compared to most of the world, has risen to obscene proportions because of these policies.

No one questions that it is a good thing to skip a meal once a week and give the money to a "feed the hungry" program. But as citizens of this nation, we must take responsibility for our national policies in order that we might use our resources more economically and productively to feed the hungry all over the world. We need to be more and more aware of the macro ethical dimension of the world's poor and hungry.

Jesus is concerned about both micro and macro ethics. He says, "Lay up for yourselves treasures in heaven" (Matt. 6:20, KJV), which suggests that one practice stewardship for the sake of his own soul. He also says, "Inasmuch as ye have done it unto one of the least of these . . . , ye have done it unto me" (Matt 25:40, KJV). Millions are starving to death every year, and Jesus says the way to love him is to use our goods in a maximum way to alleviate that hunger.

So, the problem of money is not simple. It is not evil to be rich. It is not good to be poor. But, today we Christians are being forced to find a right relationship to things. We must discover something of what it means to be stewards of all that God is giving to us personally and nationally. What we do with our things and money will say something to the world about the Lord whose name we bear.

MEMORANDUM

TO: Keith
FROM: Bruce
RE: Chapter Six—Money and Possessions

Dear Keith:

I wound up unburdening myself about our use of material things on an international scale—and I believe we've got to look at the effects of what we are doing as a nation. But the average Christian may be wading through the problems of money and possessions in a much more personal way.

What do you think money **means** spiritually? How should a Christian think about his money, and evaluate its importance in his priorities? What about money as security? And maybe some specific suggestions about the day-to-day budgeting and spending of money in a Christian home?

Bruce

P.S. Regarding the royalty advance for the book: Jarrell said, "I thought you guys were **Christians.**"

What Does Money Mean Spiritually?

Money is the golden lamp out of which we are led to believe the genie will come to fulfill our wildest fantasies. It is the universal symbol of power, of the ability to control or by-pass the hard realities of life. And it represents independence from having to do the will of other men or to relate to them—or even to God. The common people have evidently always seen money as the key to unfettered happiness. Only those few individuals (and countries) who have acquired great wealth know that it does not bring the ultimate happiness it promises. That, however, is one of the well-kept secrets of the wise old men who are the guardians of universal folklore. But how did money become this exalted symbol?

Most people do not seem to be aware of the extensive changes in civilization brought by the invention of money and the idea of accumulating private possessions.

In the early stages of the primitive world there was no "property" and therefore little need for government to force people to be fair in their handling of money and possessions. It was usual among "savages" for the person who had food to share it with people who had none, and travelers were fed at any home they chose to stop at on their way. And communities with drought, etc., were often maintained by their neighbors.[1] If a man sat down to eat in the jungle he was expected to call loudly for someone to come to share it with him, before he could rightly eat alone.[2]

With the coming of tools, weapons, agriculture, and plenty to eat, however, came trade. Then the symbol for who was the greatest, the most powerful, was economic wealth instead of physical prowess. So economic individualism and pride of wealth were married. And their offspring are the financial princes of history.

The simple communism of the savage, which seemed so attractive, virtually disappeared. As Will Durant said, "When abundance comes, and the danger subsides, social cohesion is lessened, and individualism increases; communism ends where luxury begins."[3]

And since Christians believe that man's greatest sin is his pride —his tendency to try to become number one or replace God in his own personal world—the amassing of money as a symbol of power and status was inevitable as man became an economic creature.

By the time of Jesus' ministry in Palestine, money and possessions in the Roman world had become the symbols of independence for one's self and of power over his neighbors' lives and destinies. And Jesus saw the love of money as a very dangerous thing for a Christian—since he was to love God with all his heart and his neighbor as himself. The Christian was not to lord it over other people as the Gentiles and people with power tended to do. (See Matt. 22:37–40 and 20:25 ff.) If what I have been saying is true about the danger of using money as an expression of pride, then an expanded translation of the apostle's statement concerning money might be: "The excessive love of any power and control over people's destinies is the root of all evil." It just happens that money is the universal symbol of such power.

How Should a Christian Think about Money and Possessions in an Affluent Society?

For the Christian, then, money *itself* is not evil. And the way we *feel about it* and *use* it tell whether it will be a creative or destructive force in our hands. As Gertrude Behanna, who gave away her own personal fortune, once said, "Money is like bricks: you can slug people with them or use them to build hospitals." But for those of us who do not give away all our possessions, there is a great tendency to put off even examining our true feelings about money. At least this is certainly true of me.

Most of us must work to earn money—but how much? How can we sensibly evaluate how much we should try to make and whether or not we are hooked by our money and possessions?

I have to smile when I hear wealthy people say that money doesn't mean anything to them. Augustine commented that when we have plenty of money and possessions "we think we love them not; but when they begin to depart, then we discover what kind of persons we are." The truth seems to be that we tend to be unaware of how much we depend on our material possessions.

Checking Our Values

One way of checking our relative values is to see how we use our time. Many modern psychologists would agree with Jesus in saying that what we do with our time and energy determines not only our conscious but our unconscious goals and values. Jung pointed out that "observing someone closely for a period of time to see what he does yields quite a fair picture of his relative values. If he spends more time reading than he does playing cards, then it can be assumed that reading is more highly valued than card playing." [4]

Do you spend almost all your time working for money and position to the neglect of your family, your prayers, your non-professional relationships with people? And how about your checkbook stubs? These can be a good barometer of our true sense of values. What do you spend your money for—particularly that not used for necessities?

A denomination can tell a lot about its priorities and values by examining its institutional check stubs. For instance, if a church spends 95 percent of its budget on maintaining its own building and programs, this also reveals what it really thinks about "feeding the hungry," etc. And an individual Christian family can go through its check stubs and come up with a pretty fair idea about what is really important in its priorities.

If you think this is uncomfortable to *read* as a Christian, you ought to try to *write* it—given the way I have spent money these past two years. I am reevaluating my own priorities at this time in my life—and it is very painful.

Money and Security

For many people money represents emotional security. Until a man knows that he can take care of his family's basic material needs, he may not rest easily. And this is certainly a legitimate financial goal in an economic system like ours.

Carl Jung said that man has two aims. The first is the natural aim, the begetting of children and the business of protecting the brood. To this phase of life belongs the acquisition of money and social place. When this aim has been reached, a new phase of life begins: the cultural aim. To find a spiritual goal that points beyond the purely natural man and his worldly existence *"is an absolute necessity for the health of the soul at this stage in life."* [5]

The problem with many of us in our Madison-Avenue-made world is that in our insecurity we either overspend or use our growing *net worth* as a means of trying to prove our *human worth*.

Thousands of people frantically keep trying to make more money all their lives, without ever even becoming consciously aware of the need for the *transition* from material to cultural or spiritual aims. Many people feel strange restless stirrings when their kids are about raised, but they interpret these to mean that they are in the wrong vocation or that they married the wrong person. So they may get divorced or indulge in sexual adventures to try to quiet the urgent voice that tells them in their very bones that "there is more to life than they have found in 'making and spending.' And the time to begin finding it is *now!"*

This time of life for the couple who have found a certain amount of economic security (either through work or inheritance) can be very rough, unless they can find security on a spiritual adventure.

Many marriages are being saved in America today as both partners find a new basis for unity in a common commitment to God and his purposes in the world. If a couple embarks on a new spiritual adventure together, then each may begin to discover new meaning and new priorities regarding his or her place in the secular world. The business person, doctor, teacher, or housewife may find a new role in helping others to discover themselves as persons, for example. Then the presence or absence of a lot of money may fade and become a less important factor in the basic security system of the individual or couple.

Some Suggestions about the Nitty-Gritty

Having done some marriage counseling (and having been married over twenty-five years), I am continually reminded of how much conflict in marriages (of all ages) comes about as the result of arguments over how a family's money is being spent. Much of this conflict results from a lack of even the simplest kind of communication regarding family financial management. So I am going to get specific for those of you who would like to find a more harmonious way to handle the daily allocations of your personal family finances. To do this, I am reproducing the following letter and reply:

Dear Keith:

My wife and I argue over money every month when the time comes to reconcile the bank statement. We have an adequate income with money to spare and we finally got our tithe up to ten percent. But I get furious and uptight when she buys some nonessential knickknack. When I ask about a check she's written, she hits the ceiling and gets very defensive. We wind up furious, but I can't seem to stop worrying about this. And she doesn't seem to worry enough. Every month at checkbook time the same plot unfolds to the little scene I just described, and it's miserable. What's happening at our house? Got any ideas?   P.M.

Dear P.M.,

Naturally I can't know what's happening at your house. I have enough trouble trying to figure out what's happening at our house. But several things came to mind as I read and re-read your letter.

Obviously it is very helpful if a Christian couple feels that any money in their possession is a gift from God and that they are stewards, not owners of it. This has helped me; but I realize that this *feeling* about money is also a gift from God which I did not have for much of my life. Having said that, there are several specific insights I've found helpful:

Many psychologists believe that our reactions to spending money stem from our very early training—even as early as our potty training. Thus, one could develop as a withholding, less-verbal, nonspending (anal type) person. Whereas, another might develop a giving, verbal, easy-spending (oral type) personality.

And since we often marry those whose personalities complement ours, being attracted by characteristics we feel we lack, "saving" people often marry "spenders." What may happen is that the saving spouse (who saves because it is part of his or her basic security system) is threatened by the spending mate who feels no compulsion to save.

But a saver can learn to trigger a bunch of strong guilt feelings by challenging a spender on some seemingly frivolous expenditure. Also, since money is a symbol of power as well as security, many marital arguments about its use have more to do with a deeper question concerning who's going to make the decisions than with how much is spent on what.

This is a difficult thing to write about because each family has a unique income situation. And our adjustments may not be appropriate to anyone else. Furthermore, we have used different financial plans over the years. But here are a couple of things we've tried which have been helpful when it got especially difficult at checkbook time:

1. The two of us figured out a budget (by going through the previous year's checks) and determined which bills and expenses Mary Allen might logically pay and which things I more naturally kept track of. Then we opened a new checking account in her name and deposited a check each month for the amount of her part of the budget. I continued to pay certain bills out of the original account. This having two accounts helped at once, since we balanced our checking accounts separately.

2. We found that we had to add a miscellaneous category to her part of the budget to avoid overdrawing because of legitimate but unforeseen reasons.

3. For several years after we made the budget and adjusted it annually, I thought things were going very well. But Mary Allen felt frustrated. Although she could charge certain nonessentials or buy them under "miscellaneous," she felt guilty if she bought some small frivolous item "just because."

4. So we finally added a small "nonaccountable" category to her part of the budget. Now she can buy a few things she doesn't need with no feelings of guilt.

These small adjustments have done wonders for our financial discussions. I realize that each couple is different and has a different (or really two different) life situations to face.* And I also know that none of this may be helpful because arguments about money in marriage are often actually arguments about other problems which are disguised.

You may not think these suggestions are very "spiritual" but they have certainly helped us relate better as a family.

Keith Miller

P.S. By the way, the above described simple adjustments have only taken us twenty-five years to work out!

In such a brief space there are too few pages even to mention all the issues we have faced regarding money and possessions. The question of tithing—should one start with a small percentage of

---

*I am also aware that many people do not have enough money for even the bare essentials. But a careful look at *how* the family's money is being spent can still be a helpful experience.

Money and Possessions / 127

one's income (as we did), and work up to ten percent or more, or start with ten? How much to the church and how much to other institutions and individuals? What to do when one mate wants to tithe and the other doesn't? What about long-range planning, saving and investing for children's education, and your own retirement? How to give money away intelligently? All these questions are vital, or can be, to the Christian family who really want to be good stewards of their money and possessions in an affluent society.

We have not solved some of these issues in our home. And those we have "solved" once must be reexamined when our financial picture changes.

I do know that when I am able to commit my *whole* life and future to God, on those days problems concerning the use of money do not seem nearly as important—or as impossible.

Chapter Seven

Power

MEMORANDUM

TO: Bruce
FROM: Keith
RE: Chapter Seven—Power

Dear Bruce:

This is another subject which is often either ducked or oversimplified by Christians. I've seen big blustering church officers chopped down in public with an acid look from a wife who is a "quiet and gentle" white-haired lady. Power is everywhere in the church and yet we often seem so powerless as compared to non-Christian people and institutions, because we act so weak and humble.

How about talking some concerning the way you see power in relationships. In what ways do you view life as a power struggle? How is power dispensed or acquired? And what is the greatest power any individual can seek?

Keith

Life Is a Power Struggle

In every marriage the simplest decision can evolve into a power struggle. While dressing to go out to dinner, a wife may say, "What should I wear, honey, the blue dress or the green one?" Now the husband doesn't really care which dress she wears. He likes both of them, and thinks she always looks beautiful when she goes out. But, lest he be accused of disinterest or lack of love, he studies the situation for a few seconds and says, "I think I like the blue one better." Later as they leave the house to keep their date he notices she is wearing the green one!

In a sense, all of life is a power struggle. And sex, wealth, fame, position, and beauty are some of the factors in the equation that ultimately add up to "power." In the family setting this struggle emerges when a child is still very young. Frequently, admonitions to "eat," "go potty," or "stop that" are met with clenched fists and howls of anger.

As parents, we do not give up this power struggle even when our children are grown. In all probability, our techniques will change, and we may come to see that one of the most effective ploys in getting the upper hand involves making the other person feel guilty. We've all seen this demonstrated again and again in our families. But one writer said it so well through the words of his mother who evidently was a master guilt-producer: "I'll just stop breathing so there will be more air in this room for you, dear!"

To recognize this universal power struggle, let's focus on the way power works in a person-to-person dimension. I was in the Kansas City airport recently waiting for a flight when an older couple edged up to the ticket line. Their clothes and luggage showed them to be quite well-to-do. In words that were barely audible and with eyes flashing, the woman directed her husband's every move—telling him precisely where to stand and what to do. At her carping insistence he cut into the line ahead of most of us, but he was extremely agitated and embarrassed. After a few moments his sense of decency forced him to retreat to the end of the line in spite of her contempt and fury.

Since they were on my plane, I continued to watch the extension of this sad drama until they finally disembarked. This was a stark and obvious portrayal of the power game. And I would say that the husband was as much a part of the game as the wife. I discovered later in a short conversation with him that he had been a business tycoon in years past, running thousands of employees, but now he accepted his wife's domination quite docilely. Somehow his role with her must have met a need in him, just as her ability to maneuver and boss him apparently fulfilled something in her.

The late Abraham Maslow studied married couples for years and was convinced that the source of most conflict between husbands and wives was the question of which mate was to dominate the other. He felt that problems having to do with money, children, sex, recreation, etc., were all merely surface manifestations of this fundamental battle for dominance.

The couple at the airport, as bizarre as their behavior seemed, had evidently settled that conflict in a way which met both their needs. In most marriages the dynamics in the area of power are not so obvious. In his book *The Strong and the Weak*,[1] Paul Tournier suggests that in marriage there is no distinction between the strong partner and the weak one. Both are involved in a power struggle, but the weak use different weapons. The strong person may be demanding, nagging, and aggressive while the weak person may sulk, withdraw, behave irresponsibly, or even resort to illness or threats of suicide. But all of these behaviors are blatant attempts to dominate the other person in the power play.

In understanding ourselves and our relationship to God, it is helpful to realize the function of power in every relationship. Some people hate power and call it evil because they basically hated their powerful father or mother. Therefore, any person who is an authority—any "boss," teacher, or committee chairman—is suspect and certainly evil. "Powerful people can't be good people," in their eyes.

On the other hand, there are others who feel that power is good. They love their parents. Therefore, all mommies and daddies, politicians, pastors, and bosses are basically good. These people aspire to being powerful because that is the same thing as being good.

But power is not good or bad. Power is amoral and only as

good or as bad as the use to which it is put. Power can become immoral when people do not use the obvious power that they have for the right end. Egil Krogh, one of the defendants in the Watergate trial, excused his behavior on the grounds that he was simply "following orders." But this is exactly what the people who worked in the death camps in Nazi Germany said. A more subtle charge in regard to the misuse of power has been leveled against the pope in World War II. Some people believe that he had the power to prevent the murder of millions of Jews and simply did nothing. This, they have claimed, is immoral. More recently, Billy Graham has been under attack in some quarters because he was a close friend of former President Nixon and might have used his influence to bring a swifter end to the war in Vietnam.

Different Ways to Acquire Power

But there are no innocent parties in the universal power struggle. There are many kinds of power. And each of us is responsible for the way we exercise the power that we have in the public domain as well as in our private affairs. In recent months I have come to see that there are at least two different kinds of power that all of us must deal with. There is, first, the power conferred by society through jobs and titles. It is the power of a politician or a policeman or a teacher, of a soldier or commanding officer on the battlefield, or of an executive or boss in business. Obviously, to have this kind of power and to use it wrongly or not to use it at all is immoral. Almost all of us who have been entrusted with this type of power at various times in our lives stand guilty of having used it unwisely, unjustly, or not at all.

Second, there is the illusion of power, which we might call "assumed power." Leadership is often based on the active premise that the illusion of power can be more important than conferred power. Life is full of examples of this kind of power. A small Jewish rabbi named Paul defied the authorities, and his missionary efforts spread a movement in the name of Jesus of Nazareth which has lasted two thousand years. Ralph Nader took on General Motors and many of the large corporations in our country. With no power base in the beginning, he has brought about incredible changes in our way of life—and he is not finished yet! Saul Alinsky went to the "helpless" poor of our land and organized them into power groups to break tyranny in their own towns.

My godmother was a medical doctor in Chicago. She was a

Swedish immigrant who had put herself through nurse's training, medical school, and even law school! Though an agnostic, she gave much of her time to free medical work in clinics. One day this remarkable lady stepped off the elevated train at Wilson Avenue and saw a filthy street stretching out for several blocks. Incensed, she walked into every shop, restaurant, and store along those two blocks on both sides of the street. "How dare you allow this?" she asked, confronting the shop owner or manager with the sorry condition of "his" street. Each one protested his innocence, saying he couldn't fight city hall and that garbage pick-up and street-cleaning services were inadequate. However, many weeks later I noticed that street was swept clean and that each shop owner seemed to be caring for the portion in front of his shop.

For many years my wife has considered it her personal duty to stop street fights, especially where the odds are totally unequal: an older boy beating a younger one, or one child being mistreated or abused by a number of others. Driving by, she stops the car and leaps into the fray, with words like, "Here now, stop that immediately. What's your name?" Without exception, the kids desist and disband. My wife has no legal authority over those children, but because she assumes power, power is given to her.

I think much of life is like this. We *can* fight city hall! Certainly God has given power to all of his believers. Some have real power but all of us can assume power which in the end may become the real thing.

I recently read a letter that Henry IV of France wrote to his friend Crillon, who had failed to appear for a critical battle. "Go hang yourself, brave Crillon," the letter reads, "We fought at Aques and you were not there." Well, as Christians if we have not righted some wrongs and lifted some burdens in some way in our lifetime, then, as Crillon, we stand condemned, by God, by our fellowmen . . . and by our own conscience.

Power over Self

But perhaps the type of power we most need to understand and explore is the power that each person has over his own life. One of the most interesting revolutions in modern psychiatry and psychology is the rediscovery of the human will. The power I have to change myself has been minimized in the past. Man has been seen as a victim of his environment, his subconscious, and his conditioning. One psychiatrist in Italy has said that the non-recognition of the human will is the scandal of modern psychology. Dr. Aubert, of Burrswood Hospital in England, told a workshop: "Conventional psychiatry under the influence of the behaviorist and Freudian schools has reduced the area of man's free will almost to nothing, making him little more than the helpless victim of instinctual drives, conditioned reflexes, heredity, environment, physiology, and so on."

The emphasis on the will and the insistence that people take responsibility for themselves comes from many sources today. Listen to what William Schutz, author of *Here Comes Everybody*,[2] said in a workshop recently: "One of the big jobs of encounter is to put people in touch with the fact that their lives are their responsibility and their choice. And I think that's the big turn-around. If people can get to that realization, that's a tremendous liberation. And at that point when you realize that everything that's happening to you is what you're doing in the first place, it sounds awful. It sounds like, 'Oh, my God. I have to be responsible for being near-sighted and for having a cold and for all the terrible things that people did to me, for breaking my arm and everything.' Well, if you think about it for awhile, that gives you power because if you did it, you can change it. You don't have to wait now for the world to change or for society to change or whatever. It's up to you."

William Glasser, discussing reality therapy with a group of us in Baltimore, said, "There is nothing that undercuts effective living more than excuses. If you want to try something, start on Monday and try to live five days of your life without excusing anything you do. Just live a whole week without excusing anything. If you're late and people ask what happened, just say, 'I'm late because I am incompetent.' There is no other reason, so you may as well tell the truth. You'll only say that once and you won't be late for a long, long time after that. If someone asks, 'Why didn't you do it?' say 'Because I didn't want to,' if that is the truth. But most of the things people are asking you about you've got control over. And if it isn't exercised, say that you're incompetent, you're lazy."

As Glasser points out, we can have choices about the direction of our lives. The problem is that so often we choose to pretend that we have no power over our lives. Glasser had some further things to say about how to help people take responsibility for themselves. A turning point came in his own training when he asked his superior how to begin to help people in a mental hospital. His teacher said, "First you teach them to tie their shoes." Apparently, there is no place where you see more untied shoes than in a mental hospital. This is a sign that the patient has given up responsibility for himself. Glasser's teacher was saying that in working with a patient the first step is to help him begin to do the thing every well person does—which in this case is to tie his shoes. Beginning with this simple act, the patient begins to understand that he is not a victim of other people's actions but of his own choices and that he can change his choices by beginning to do simple, responsible things.

And so we see that this power over self can perhaps be the most creative use of power. The power that others use to manipulate me in relationships or the power exerted on me through groups can be overcome by my power over myself. I can even choose to be happy. No one can take away from me my right to be happy. I am responsible for myself. And what is wrong with me as well as what is right with me is a result of my own choices. Finally, I believe that God can be a participant in those choices. The feeling that one is loved and has worth in the eyes of the Supreme Being can give us courage to live in this radically courageous way full of pitfalls and failures.

I can exercise power over myself and begin to take responsibility for who I am. At a beginning level, I can start to tie my shoes, and I can move on up to the point of choosing a worthy goal for my life, something to live for and to die for. In exercising this power I become someone of worth, whose life has meaning, and who can help other people to find a creative use of power.

MEMORANDUM

TO: Keith
FROM: Bruce
RE: Chapter Seven—Power

Dear Keith:
    In reading over my material, I realize that I haven't tied power into its source: God. I have a lot of trouble telling people (and understanding) about the unique nature of God's power. I know that from the beginning of the biblical story, he has given men "power from on high" which has allowed them to do remarkable things. But what is the usefulness of that power? Is it any different in the way it works from political or physical power? What are the characteristics of God's kind of power? And how do you think people trying to live the adventure of faith can get and use that power in their life together?
                                                        Bruce

In one sense the whole drama which sweeps through the Old and New Testaments is the story of a power struggle, illustrated by hundreds of lesser power struggles in the lives and writings of the biblical characters.

The earliest accounts of creation in Genesis portray the first man and his mate as being happily located in a virtual paradise. But this was not enough for them. They realized that God knew something, had something, that they didn't and this knowledge gave him power they did not have. So man's classic sin was committed when he tried to steal the wisdom and power of the place of God for himself. And since we were made with a certain freedom to choose, we seem to have chosen ever since to try to get power or acclaim, or preference, over each other and subtly even over God. Look at Cain and Abel, Jacob and Esau, Joseph and his brothers, Aaron and Moses, clear through to Jesus' disciples arguing about who was to sit on the right hand and who on the left in the coming Kingdom.

Two Kinds of Power

Throughout the dramatic biblical accounts, two kinds of power are seen pitted against each other. On one side was materially based power, consisting of physical superiority (Pharaoh's armies against the unarmed Hebrews, the armored Philistine giant Goliath against the practically naked shepherd boy David, armed only with a slingshot, etc.).

On the side opposing the material strength was the power of God which consisted of a certain intangible wisdom and perception only *visible* in its *results*.

The numerical and physical balance of power recognized by both contestants or armies in the biblical struggles was on the side *opposing* God's people.* And victory for the Hebrews almost always appeared to be impossible from the standpoint of any reasonable human criteria of power.

---

* Some exceptions were when God's people had become cocky and unfaithful; then they were defeated by people with smaller numbers and material power (e.g., the people of Ai after the battle of Jericho).

The settled and relatively sophisticated Philistines were an *entire metallic age* ahead of the nomadic Hebrews as they moved into Palestine to try to conquer it. That's not quite equivalent to a nation with atomic weaponry defending itself against one with only conventional weapons, but historically it may not have seemed all that different either—if you were the people without the newer equipment. Later we see Gideon with his three hundred men against the many peoples of the Midianites: "they came up with their herds and their tents, like a swarm of locusts; they and their camels were past counting. They had come into the land and laid it waste" (Judg. 6:5, margin, NEB).

And I suppose the classic picture of God's people being a long shot to succeed came much later. After the life and death of Jesus, a group of eleven defeated men gathered in Galilee—the equivalent of a backwoods county seat in the Texas desert. They had already proved they were not heroic by deserting Jesus (Matt. 26:56). And he had been disgracefully and publicly abused and hanged (crucified).

This sad little group had no material, ecclesiastical, or political power base. And here was Jesus before them. He had come back, still alone and unarmed, and was about to leave them again. He was calmly giving them the assignment to "make disciples of all nations" and to tell *all* people to do with their lives what Jesus had instructed the disciples to do. If we can get an objective picture of this exhausted and rejected ragtag group of eleven middle-class men—with no formal training in either theology or communication—being given the assignment to *change the entire world's ideas about God,* when this involved political confrontation and treason against the government—it is almost funny. And not only that, but they were to win the world's *total spiritual allegiance* to a carpenter from a hick town who was never even ordained by the church (see Matt. 28:16–20). The presumption of Jesus' command is almost pathetic.

And yet in less than three hundred years, the gospel of Jesus became the official religion of the Roman world, since it evidently appeared to the Emperor Constantine to be the only force powerful enough to bind the empire together.

Characteristics of God's Kind of Power

How could this be? What are the dynamics of this apparently illogical power of God which outlasts armies and empires?

Invisible. First, one of the primary characteristics of God's power—which I've already mentioned—is that it is evidently *not measurable in material terms*—numbers or size—as almost all other accumulated power seems to be. God's power, as compared to other socio-political power, is *invisible.* And the invisible nature of this power makes it a ridiculous and nonviable choice for a materialist or a materialistic government (e.g., who but a fool would attack an army of thousands with three hundred men?).

Different Perception. But the immeasurable nature of God's power also gives it its great tactical advantage: surprise. For the essence of what God seems to give to those he wants to use in a powerful way in the world is a kind of broader and clearer *perception* of the conflict situation. This perception takes in not only the statistical measure of the opposing forces, but the human weaknesses, the personal vulnerabilities, the fears and expectations of the opposing leaders and their men. And as a result of his broader perception, God's man for the hour was given a clever tactical plan which forced the larger opponent to fight at a great disadvantage on God's terms.

Enormous motivation is provided God's leaders by the fact that they also see beyond the immediate and material dimensions of the conflict to the deeper moral and spiritual issues pertaining to the contestants' relationship to God and his will.

I examined the biblical accounts of the encounters of "God's people" with nations using material power. And I saw that the victories over superior numbers could be accounted for by this unique kind of cleverness which the biblical authors called "wisdom."* David's realization that he could defeat Goliath with a stone rather than by fighting him on the usual military terms is an example. Or Gideon's trick of giving each of his three hundred men a trumpet and an empty pitcher with a torch in it. They surrounded the enemy at night, blew the trumpets, and broke the pitchers. In the confusion which followed, the various elements of the invading army fought each other and Gideon's men won. (See 1 Samuel 17 and Judges 7.)

Prior Commitment. But even though it was true that one could account for the victory of God's people in terms of wisdom or cleverness, this *wisdom* was always described as coming from God

---

* The Hebrew word *wisdom* meant more nearly our word *cleverness.* See a classic example of Solomon's "wisdom" in 1 Kings 3:16–28.

to a man chosen by him for the occasion. And the wisdom came just as it was needed—most often *after* the receiver of it *had already committed himself totally to the battle.*

So I began to realize that perhaps God's sort of power is channeled through the life of a man or woman *already* totally committed to God's cause. This power often takes the form of a deeper perceiving and understanding of a seemingly impossible situation (if viewed from a rational-materialist point of view). And with this new perception of the situation may come a simple but profound solution, different from those usually tried by the power structure in question. This would be true of Moses, Deborah, David, Amos, Paul, Martin Luther, clear down to Martin Luther King, and beyond. And of course their prototype and model was Jesus Christ.

The Doorway to Power: Death?

Where do the people who use God's sort of power in public crises get the courage to use invisible strength in the face of massive governments, churches, and armies? And how does the power of an inspired leader communicate itself to his followers?

I think the answer to both questions may be in the same direction. A strange part of the Adam and Eve story occurs in the dialogue between Eve and the serpent. She is told that God forbade them to eat the fruit of the tree of knowledge, because they would then be in the "God class" of power and wisdom. And the warning concerning the fruit indicated that if they did start competing with God in this way they would *die.*

So from the beginning *death* has been the great power of God which man could not contend with—at least indefinitely. And when man gains material and political power, the greatest weapon he can hold over his opponent's head is the threat of killing him. So the threat of death keeps the powerful in power—one way or the other.

But Jesus Christ came along and said he was bringing in a new kind of kingdom with a different sort of power. He gave his followers a secret key to the greatest kind of power for a human being: *a way to transcend death—the world's ultimate power weapon!*

Let us say a man or woman commits his life to Jesus Christ as totally as he can. Then he is drawn to a conflict caused by man's sin or power lust. When he commits himself to the victims involved, he may then receive a perception and understanding of the total problem and its relation to those in power which other people cannot (or dare not) see. And with what appears to be amazing courage, he confronts the power structure.

At first the powerful opponents are contemptuous and let God's man speak, for there is no visible material threat. But then they see that he has seen their unrighteousness and that he is evidently *not afraid to die!*

And paradoxically, it is at about this point that followers begin to come out of the woodwork. For the common people realize that this person of God is tied into a power or security greater than that which they knew. So they listen to him and many follow and identify with him. They see a fearlessness and a creative strength which, unlike the world's power, is *available to people like themselves!* The mighty opponents see this, and realize they are dealing with a very dangerous person, though they do not understand the nature of his power base. For before them stands one with no army nor electorate who may destroy their whole structure. He can see their vulnerability and is not afraid of their most dangerous weapon. So they must directly or indirectly destroy him—and those who are afraid of losing their power usually do destroy the prophets. But by the time they get around to it, a seed may have been planted in the crack made by the impact of the prophet's life against the unjust power structure. And in a few years that seed may grow and split the greatest of institutions apart. Look at St. Francis. Look at Luther. Look at Wesley. Look at Martin Luther King. Whatever you may think about their personal lives or even their theological ideas, God gave them power to use for him in the world.

How Do We Get God's Power?

How would an ordinary Christian begin to live in such a way that he might learn to open himself to God's power, which includes Christ's courage and perception? From reading the Scriptures and the church's history, one thing seems certain: prophets and saints are not made in a crisis or by waiting around hoping God will "give them a chance." As Donn Moomaw, a great all-American linebacker, once told me, "A football team is not made or broken on the six-inch line with ten seconds to go. It is only *revealed!*" I do not believe the true nature of a Christian's life is made or broken in a crisis. The behavior revealed in a crisis is the product of months or years of prayer, reading the Scriptures, trying to live in relation to God and his people in the cauldron of daily life. Then, if the public call of God comes, the Christian is simply doing what he has been doing all along—trying to live a free and creative life and create conditions so that other people can. Of course in a "crisis" he may be doing these things on a much larger and more public stage. But his basic relationship to God doesn't change.

And where did we Christians get the authority to use God's full arsenal of power in the world? When Jesus at the last was standing empty-handed on the hill in Galilee sending the eleven disciples forth in his name to conquer the world, he is reported to have passed on to them one useful gift which is often ignored because it was invisible. He said he had been given God's full authority "in heaven and on earth." And that he would be with them always—bringing them God's power.

Chapter Eight

Christian Sexuality

MEMORANDUM

TO: Bruce
FROM: Keith
RE: Chapter Eight—Christian Sexuality

Dear Bruce:

Although the world seems to be full of literature about sexual behavior these days, I almost never see anything **specific** being written by people who are writing **as Christians trying to live the adventure of faith.** Writers often switch into their roles as psychologists or sociologists, and we are left wondering what they think about sex as husbands, wives, or simply persons who are committed to Christ.

Let's break out of that mold in this chapter. I've heard you speak frankly about a Christian view of sex which makes real sense to me. Why don't you include at least some of these questions: What are some ways to look at sexuality? What about sex and personhood? And how about dealing with some of the common questions Christians ask concerning premarital sex, legitimate positions for intercourse for married Christians, frequency, extramarital sex, divorce, erotic literature, staying single, homosexuality, masturbation, and perhaps something of the overall biblical view of sex.

Keith

I've encountered many mature, responsible Christians these days who are reading books about sex. One couple, following directions in one of the latest volumes, was trying to discover new erogenous zones. "Kissing my wife's big toe probably would have worked," the husband reported, "if we both hadn't started laughing!"

I think this new and acceptable kind of interest in sex is a healthy change for most of us Christians. No one needs to be more enlightened about sex than those of us who have had a Christian upbringing. Many of us have been victims of a lot of wrong thinking. I think this accounts for the tremendous interest in a variety of new books on the subject. Books like *The Joy of Sex* and a number of companion volumes about "him," "her," and "them" have found a wide audience among all kinds of people—young, middle-aged, and older—including the most serious Christians. Beyond that, the simple issue of sex education in the public schools has caused a furor everywhere, even in the most enlightened communities. If you have attended any of these local school board meetings, then you know that feelings about sex are strong, ignorance on the subject is vast and often hidden under the guise of faith and morality.

Different Ways to Look at Sex

It seems to me that currently there are three general views of sex, two of them widespread and basically unhealthy. The first is that *sex is a necessary evil*. In the church we have seen this as a glorification of celibacy as over against the married state. The implication is that if one were really "Christian," he could live with a minimum of sex in his life, or none at all. It's surprising to find this ancient philosophy popping up today on the secular scene. Ratings for movies are determined by the degree of nudity portrayed. A movie showing a bare breast or bottom becomes an R movie even though there may be no overt sex or violence in it. But a movie full of violence and implicit sex may get a PG rating, providing there is no nudity.

A second point of view maintains that *sex is a simple biological function and meant to be enjoyed*. In classic literature (books like *The Decameron* and *Canterbury Tales*) we find much in the medieval and eighteenth-century traditions that would indicate great numbers of people practicing uninhibited, bawdy sex. In more recent times, the Playboy philosophy is a very sophisticated presentation of irresponsible sex. Promiscuous intercourse is to be enjoyed just as one enjoys a meal, a bath, or a good night's sleep.

The seeds of this kind of sexual philosophy were sown by Freud who reacted, and rightly, against the Victorian view that sex was a necessary evil and therefore to be repressed. But Freud's theory that man suffered neuroses because he could not give free rein to his sexual drives has done irreparable harm, especially to Christians who have sought new attitudes through psychoanalysis.

There is a third view of sex especially applicable for Christians which is that *sex is good and to be enjoyed but always in the context of responsibility*. Christians ought to be sexy. Sex is not a necessary evil but a gift given by God to enjoy. God has also given certain rules that make us responsible for others and for ourselves. Within these confines, sex is a powerful and wonderful gift to be celebrated.

In helping someone else find all that he is meant to be by God in the area of sexuality, one needs to understand which of these three basic attitudes is his—realizing that there are many gradations and combinations of the three views mentioned. To help a person change his basic attitude about sex is more important than to help him solve a particular problem in this area.

Sex and Personhood

There is another dimension of sex which is undergoing drastic change in our time. This is the distinction between sex and personhood. In our society our sex largely determines our culturally assigned role. There are male and female virtues, male and female talents, male and female reactions, all predetermined. In point of fact, we have assumed there is a basic male personality and a basic female personality.

What is the biblical view of the male/female role? Certainly God created two sexes, male and female, and called them good and meant them for one another. In the Old Testament and even in the New, the woman's role is clearly defined as inferior to that of the man. But I think we need to understand that the biblical revelation came at a time when slavery was acceptable, Samaritans were judged inferior, and live animals and even people were killed to placate God. All of this occurred because man did not know any better.

How amazing that Paul, at the same time he spoke of women being silent in church and submissive to men, also said, by the inspiration of the Holy Spirit, that in Christ there is neither male nor female, only a new creation. The cultural stereotypes were so ingrained, I'm not sure Paul even knew the far-reaching implications of what he was saying. But I believe with all my heart that he was prophetic in speaking of the time to come when we will stop assigning certain personality roles to sexes. We are finally beyond trying to make a left-handed child right-handed, so we ought to stop assuming that a boy who is basically aesthetic or artistic or gentle is not a man. In the same way, women who are basically aggressive, competent managers and organizers should not be made to feel that they are less than feminine.

This strict assignment of roles to the sexes may account for the great number of people who become homosexuals or lesbians. A man feels so ashamed of being effeminate that he stops competing with men and enters into a female world. The same reversal can take place in a woman's experience. It would be far healthier, it seems to me, were we to suggest that there might be a creative union between a female with masculine psychological tendencies and a male with feminine tendencies. In point of fact, I know a number of couples like this who seem to have mature and healthy marriages.

In our own marriage my wife is more capable of handling certain matters which are traditionally considered the male prerogative (checkbook and income taxes). At first it was difficult to accept this and not feel threatened. But liberation is coming and it feels good for me not to have to defend my maleness but simply to be a person married to a person. It is an adventure to enjoy our personhood and our sexuality and our different gifts—even though it is not always easy.

Some Common Questions about Sex

Let's look now at some of the questions that come up in the area of sex. In thinking about our sexuality, let's explore some of the most common areas of concern and see how we can view ourselves and others in the light of God's potential for each one of us.

1. What about premarital sex? This is the question I am asked most commonly today in meetings with young people. In our age of so-called sexual liberation, this question is bound to come up. In the past the church's main arguments against premarital sex were the risk of pregnancy and venereal disease. Since science has greatly lessened these two threats, we are now obliged to find a genuinely biblical reason for chastity.

When I grew up, it was often assumed that premarital sex was as wrong as adultery and that the Bible explicitly said so. It is true that the Bible is clear about adultery, but it does not seem to be as explicit about premarital sex. The sixth chapter of 1 Corinthians suggests, however, that any time two people have intercourse, these two people become one in body, mind, and spirit. Far from being dirty or evil, sex at the point of intercourse is so powerful that you become one with another person. The obvious implication is that one cannot have this experience with many people, or even with several people, without violating himself as well as the others. This seems to me an implicit case for premarital chastity.

Many people have been sold on the idea of premarital sex in order to avoid coming to the honeymoon as an amateur. If the purpose of a honeymoon is for two experts to come and demonstrate their techniques on each other, then I suppose this would make sense. But I think the most exciting thing about a honeymoon is that two people come together as amateurs and begin the process of learning together what it means to become one body, one mind, and one spirit. If this is true, then sexual experience before marriage works against the whole wonder of what God has planned for a marriage. What couples might do is to explore together before marriage their *attitudes* about sex. Do they have the same preconceptions about exploration and fulfillment on the sexual adventure in marriage?

Interestingly, I have never talked to a single married couple who said they were grateful for their premarital experience. Marriage is a time for learning together how to please one another and how to fulfill one another. No amount of experience can prepare you adequately for this.

2. What about sex in marriage? Marriage is more than sex, but any marriage that does not include an active and healthy sex life is very likely in for trouble. Sex is more than a physical experience although it is certainly unequivocally physical. Even books like those of Masters and Johnson [1] that explore the world of sex, orgasm, and fulfillment seem to put sex in a very spiritual category. For example, every time they report a couple having a breakthrough in the sexual area of their marriage, it involves some kind of emotional vulnerability on the part of one or both. In other words, the book seems to affirm what every Christian ought to know—that sex is not the key to union but an expression of union. God intended for a man and a woman to live together in union; in the Christian culture this means marriage. The sex act is not the means to union but rather an expression of the psychic, spiritual, emotional, and mental unity in which people hold no more secrets from each other. I can think of a number of couples who have had breakthroughs in their marriage and subsequently in their sex lives when they could experience confession and openness with each other. When psychic walls come down, sex becomes a sacramental expression of union.*

3. *What positions are permissible for intercourse in marriage?* I personally believe that no position is off-limits for two people to use in making love, except where one of the persons feels violated or imposed upon or embarrassed. In other words, there is no one accepted position. We do the thing that will bring fulfillment to the other.

I'm always suspicious when someone asks about "bad" positions in a marriage counseling situation. It seems to me that if one party can find an off-limits position, then he or she can nail the other for being "perverted." Once someone begins to be legalistic in any area, the marriage becomes a very shaky affair.

Intercourse in marriage is a means of giving love and pleasure to the other, but even more, it is a way of receiving what the other is able to give. The mark of love is being able to accept what the other person is able and willing to give at that moment and, beyond accepting it, delighting in it. This goes beyond rules.

In marriage, when we read a book to discover outside authority for what positions in intercourse are permissible, or what the other person *ought* to find permissible, we may be on the way to

---

* Sexual impotency and frigidity are often the outward expression of psychic walls and emotional separation. Help by a qualified counselor can often be invaluable.

creating a tragedy where both sides are right and, therefore, both sides are wrong. Practically speaking, if I want to improve the sex life of my marriage, I would get better results by buying *The Sensuous Man* for myself than by buying *The Sensuous Woman* for my wife.

4. What about the frequency of intercourse in marriage? Just as there is no right position, there is no average frequency. When one begins to ask this question, one is often trying to find out where his or her mate is failing, either in demanding too much or in not giving enough. There will almost always be an inequality of appetite, and this in itself is part of the whole communication game in marriage. God ought to make it possible for us to enjoy being on either side of this continuing dialogue. We may find that we can meet our partner's needs sometimes, even if they exceed our own, or allow them to meet ours out of love (instead of need) when appropriate. Unfortunately, the name of the game is often power and not sex. It is illuminating to find that when one partner adopts the more passive role in a marriage, the other invariably becomes the aggressor. In other words, the role of the demanding one or the passive one is often more a psychological power play than the result of a physical sex drive.

5. What about extramarital sex? The Bible is very clear about this and speaks often and strongly against adultery. One of the original Ten Commandments is a flat "You shall not commit adultery" (Exod. 20:14). Earlier I mentioned some reasons for this prohibition. Adultery is wrong because intercourse is a means of mystical union which makes two people one. Adultery is always harmful and against God's best plan for man. But I feel that Christians have blown it up out of all proportion until it has become "the unforgivable sin." We feel much less strongly about coveting or not honoring our father and mother, for example. But the seventh commandment must be seen in perspective with the other nine. It's strange how seldom we hear of a Christian wife divorcing her husband because he doesn't honor his father and mother or because he covets his boss's job.

6. What about divorce? The Bible seems clear that divorce is wrong. But so is war, yet sometimes that is the lesser of two evils. What happens when two people find that even though they are both Christians, they cannot live together creatively? It may be that divorce is a way out for both. To stay married for the sake of the children may do irreparable harm to the children, and there is

Christian Sexuality / 153

no justification for that. To stay married in order to fulfill some law of God and destroy each other surely is not valid. Even though it is not what God planned for man, divorce may be better than staying married to someone you wish were dead—for that is murder—or continually imagining that you are married to someone else—for that is adultery.

The more important issue in any case, it seems to me, is to help a person understand what real love and responsibility would look like for him and the others involved.

7. What about erotic literature? To read erotic literature if you're a salesman in a strange motel room or a lonely widow on a cold night is stupid. It's like standing in front of a bakery window, broke and hungry. To read erotic literature when there is no legitimate means of fulfilling your sex drive is stupid. To read erotic literature when you already have so much sex drive you can't handle it is stupid. But if you are the passive partner in a marriage, it seems to me that the reading of erotic literature is not only justifiable but can be even desirable. This is not a case for erotic literature but a case for finding ways to undo some of the psychological damage done to many of us years ago so that our marriage can be more fulfilling for our partner.

8. What about the single person? The Bible certainly seems to commend the single state to many. But it warns that no one should try to live this way by sheer will power unless there is a predisposition of some kind or a special gift of God's grace in this area. In the Roman Catholic tradition it seems that the single life is esteemed as being more pious than the married life. In the Protestant tradition many have implied that the married life is better than the single life. I think both views as generalizations are nonsense. Jesus Christ came to make us whole people. It is our personhood that he is concerned about, more than our married or single state.

The loneliness of the single person is no more or less painful than the loneliness of many married people, although there is no way to know that outside of marriage. But the more important issue may be to help the single person realize that God has a fulfilling purpose for him or her—married or single. In counseling a single person who wants to get married, but is uncertain, one important thing is to help that person discover whether there are any irrational reasons or fears he or she is using to *avoid* marriage. This can prove to be liberating.

Some people are single because they have set goals that are

much too high. They are looking for a Mr. or Miss Right who will never come along and who does not exist. That person may be single because he or she has never accepted his or her own humanity and the humanity of others.

On the other hand, there are people who are single because of a great fear of rejection. I just spent a number of days at a conference also attended by a lovely single girl. At one point she could finally tell all of us that her singleness came out of this fear of being rejected. She often became emotionally involved with married men because they were clearly off-limits. To compete for single men her own age so terrified her that she retreated, loudly proclaiming to all that she loved her freedom as a single person. This young woman is now moving into a new dimension in understanding her own personhood and her own goals.

Some people are single because of their low self-esteem. They cannot believe that anybody could love them. I have known some really attractive men and women who did not date because they could not imagine anybody caring to become involved with them emotionally, let alone romantically.

To assume that people are single because of happenstance in this day and age is often naïve, though it may be true. Many single people have some other problem at work in their life. A counselor needs to help them see this and give them the support and acceptance they need to move out into freedom.

Finally, there are single people who have weighed both sides and frankly prefer their freedom to the companionship married life offers. These people have been penalized in our society. I've heard one friend lament that dinner parties can never be held for an odd number of people. She is invariably asked to come and bring a man. This says to her that she is unacceptable alone. Just as the Roman Catholic tradition has made second-class citizens of married people, so our Western Protestant tradition has made second-class citizens of single people. It is easy to forget that people have problems whatever their marital status. So let's affirm that God is for people, single or married!

9. What about the homosexual? I've already suggested that part of the problem of the homosexual will be solved when we stop assigning male and female roles to people. We need to understand that in the area of homosexuality our job is not to condemn the homosexual but to love him, have concern for him, and to help him, when this is his desire, to enter into some kind of heterosexual life where there is a hope for fulfillment. I do not know a single homosexual who is happy to be what he is. On the surface they say, "Gay is great," but underneath it's a long, tired, hard, lonely road. There are many people caught in the homosexual trap who would not be there if they could have a friend who would believe in and for them and help them accept their role but not their state.

10. What about masturbation? I think we've come a long way from the old days when it was thought that masturbation was mentally and physically harmful. Charlie Shedd, in his wonderful, whimsical book, *The Stork Is Dead,* has a chapter entitled "Masturbation: God's Gift to the Teenager." [2] This has really disturbed a number of people who cannot adjust to thinking of this old taboo as a gift. Certainly masturbation can be the way God has given for easing what seems like intolerable tension, both for the single and the married. But I don't know of anyone who practices masturbation from time to time who does not feel guilty afterwards. The happy Portnoy does not seem to exist.

Basically, it seems to me that masturbation is a way of taking one's destiny into one's own hands. For the Christian to choose masturbation as a sexual life-style may put him in the place where he says to God, "I can run my own life. I no longer trust you to provide for my sexuality. I'll do it for myself." Masturbation is not bad, but it is certainly not God's best. Where it keeps a person from relating lovingly to another person, refraining from it may be a new way of trusting God.

11. What is the biblical view of sex? I can find nothing in the Bible that implies that sex is evil. On the contrary, I find evidence that sex is good, that intercourse is good, and that marriage is good. In Genesis 1:27 we find that "God created man in his own image, . . . male and female he created them." In Genesis 1:31 we find "God saw all that he had made, and it was very good."

Even beyond that, the New Testament talks about the new fellowship called the church or the Body of Christ. And it is described in terms of a marriage, with Christ the bridegroom and us believers as the bride. Marriage and the marriage bed seem to be honored over and over again in Scripture and, indeed, used as an illustration for the most intimate relationship between Christ and his people.

Finally, we have this injunction from Paul, "To the pure all things are pure; but nothing is pure to the tainted minds of disbelievers" (Titus 1:15).

For a Christian to be married is not easy. For a Christian to be single has many problems. Whatever our state, let's learn how to celebrate God's gift of sexuality in responsible ways.

MEMORANDUM

TO: Keith
FROM: Bruce
RE: Chapter Eight—Christian Sexuality

Dear Keith:
 I remember one time we were talking about the complexity of dealing with the issue of sex in the church, and you made the comment that you thought part of the reason it's so difficult is that husbands and wives often use sex for other purposes than relating to and enjoying each other. And with regard to emotional conflicts attached to the sex act, you used the expression, "A good many people seem to be fighting their battles on the wrong battlefields."
 Would you elaborate on what you meant by statements like "using sex as a sign of success," "sex as a medium of exchange," and "sex as a battleground"? And I think it would be very helpful if you would discuss the whole question of facing adultery and possible reconciliation in Christian marriage. Also I get a lot of questions about "sex and small groups" and "What about the committed Christian and sexual lust?"

Bruce

It is one thing to read learned discourses on the function of sex in the dynamics of human personality. But it's a very different experience to *live* as a sexual being—to experience the promise, the ecstasy, the agony brought about in the inner life by the superpowerful sexual instinct! We are often so alone with our questions and doubts. Christians have, for unaccountable reasons, sometimes assumed that becoming "converted" sort of automatically does away with difficulties concerning sex. And because of our fears of being thought sinful or dirty-minded, we have virtually deleted specific questions about sex from our communication with each other as Christians. But there is untold misery in Christian homes because the parents cannot communicate their views of sex to their children. The discord and pain resulting from the fact that many marriage partners cannot discuss their sexual hopes, inhibitions, and fantasies with each other are often staggering to the counseling minister or psychologist.

It seems to be true that as complexity of thought increases in a society, control of the person by his raw instincts decreases. However, there may be some horrible surprises in store for the naïve Christian who assumes that the awesome power of the sexual instinct has disappeared simply because no one talks about it publicly after making a commitment to Christ.

Sex as "Success"

In our society sexual prowess or beauty, like money, has become for many people a symbol of personal adequacy and success. And the image of the sexually attractive female or the sexually adequate male presents an unconscious goal for the young boy or girl watching TV and reading magazines. But the advertising and pictorial portrayals are so unreal that the inexperienced young Christian is almost bound to feel inadequate or cheated when he or she marries. This is especially likely to be true if either has the Playboy attitude about how a wife or husband should perform sexually.

Unless the couple can communicate openly about their sexual feelings, there is a very good chance that, instead of going away, these suppressed feelings will turn into hostility or resentment in *another* area of the couple's relationship. For instance, they may begin to criticize each other about the way the children are being raised or the money spent. Such arguments can never be satisfactorily resolved since the battles are being fought on the wrong battlefields.

Sex as a "Medium of Exchange"

Another common misuse of sex occurs when the wife uses sexual intercourse as a weapon or a "medium of exchange"—a sort of money. Of course, this role is reversed in some homes. But the traditional game is played like this: the wife says to the husband, through her behavior, "You be a *good* boy and I'll let you have some sex," or "You've been a *bad* boy (and not pleased me today), so we are not going to make love!" or "If you will buy me that beautiful dress . . ."

In one case I know about (both parties are now dead), the deeply committed Christian husband came to me in tears of frustration. His wife was *charging him* $35.00 every time they had sexual relations. But in most situations the game never reaches such an obvious or verbal level. The power is wielded silently and sometimes even unconsciously. And because both partners are Christian and committed to monogamy, one partner often feels that the dedicated mate will not dare to "step out" on him or her. But over a period of years, using sex as a weapon or means of barter can lead to a silent bitterness and resentment which may erupt in surprising ways.

Sex as a Battleground

The counterpart of the situation just described is where the wife in a Christian home feels that all the husband really wants her for is as a sex object. He is too busy to listen to her or really be with her, but he always has time to pick up his clean shirts and take her to bed—between plane flights or committee meetings. And in this case the wife develops the frustrated bitterness.

Sometimes the two sets of circumstances just described are closely related. And sex becomes a frustrating emotionally charged experience for both parties—even though they both may enjoy it physically and basically love each other very much. But they cannot be truly intimate because the resentment hovers over the bed like an odious black cloud.

There are many other sexual games Christian couples play which keep both partners from freedom and fulfillment in their relationship. Bruce has already dealt with the necessity of open communication in marriage (without threat of retaliation or rejection) about one's own true hopes and sexual feelings. This sort of communication—with a third-party marriage counselor if necessary—may help one or both marriage partners to get over false presuppositions, or to understand a partner who has them. Then the couple may begin to relate to *each other* as unique individuals with special needs and dreams. This communication is especially important, since many sexual problems result from one mate or both unconsciously relating to the other as a parent instead of a wife or husband. Thus, as many psychologists have pointed out, there could be (emotionally) as many as four people in the marriage bed. But the sort of open communication which leads to new freedom is not easy to come by when one or both partners have been raised strictly.

Facing Adultery

But what if a frustrated and resentful wife or husband has never heard the good news that Christians are free to enjoy sex in marriage? Or what if years have gone by and because of inner pressures or loneliness and outward temptations one of the partners has succumbed to temptation and committed adultery? Often the Christian having transgressed is surprised and horrified at his own behavior because he has repressed his intentions as he moved "innocently" into the compromising situation.

What happens to the couple's lives, and particularly their sex life, when the adultery is discovered or confessed? All too often, as Bruce has suggested, adultery is treated as if it were much more horrible than transgressing any of the other Ten Commandments, and the pain, guilt, and repercussions are often magnified accordingly.

Sex and adultery mean many different things to different people. So the success of reconciliation attempts may vary from fairly quick and relatively complete to impossible and a severe psychological breakdown of the offended mate.

For instance, if a woman's identity and security are strongly wrapped up in her sexual desirability, adultery by her husband may be devastating and represent total rejection to her. Sexual desirability often means power to either sex. For instance, if inordinate masculine insecurity has driven a man to succeed or achieve power in his vocation in order to compensate for his hidden feelings of inadequacy, the affront of his wife's infidelity may be too much to bear. But in any case, where two Christians have genuinely cared for each other in marriage, the pain of betrayal and the broken trust are almost bound to be agonizing. A covenant with God has been broken as well as with that person to whom one's own life is most closely joined.

Reconciliation

However severe the hurt, the process for reconciliation always seems to be costly and roughly the same: the offended party must forgive the sinner. The sinner must of course "come home," and for ultimate healing to take place, it would seem that he must confess his sin (even if the spouse has already discovered it).

Only God can give an offended mate the grace to forgive without punishing. And forgiveness does not necessarily take away the pain, which may last for a lifetime. The return to a good relationship, personally and sexually, may be long and slow. But the process can be helped tremendously if the one hurt is aware of his or her own sin and self-centeredness. Of course, the adultery is often a symptom of deeper problems—either in the individual or in the marriage relationship. And if this is true, professional counseling can sometimes be especially helpful. One of the sad problems concerning the difficulties in the intimate "hidden" areas of life is that many Christians are too proud to get psychological help when it might give them a whole new chance in life.

Though many couples can't make it back together after adultery has been committed, many others have told me that their relationship has become stronger and more sensitive through the pain of such an experience.

Some Questions about Sex and "Living the Adventure"

Bruce has suggested that I discuss some of the common fears related to sex in the Christian community. Here are a few of the questions I've heard from concerned church leaders:

"What about the dangers of sexual intimacy in the openness of life together in small groups?"

What happens to us in the Christian community, in the Body of Christ? If sexual expression is a God-given gift of grace for the overcoming of physical and emotional loneliness between man and woman, it is inextricably bound into the gospel. For the gospel is also concerned with the overcoming of the separation of people, as well as the separation between man and God.

Both Bruce and I have talked about loneliness. And the sense of aloneness and incompleteness even in "Christian" marriages is so well known that merely to mention it is to describe it for many people.* So when a person gets converted and decides to commit his whole future to the living Christ, he begins to feel the release from the awful threat of a lonely and meaningless future. He meets other radiant, changing Christians in small groups. Together, they begin to find freedom and acceptance, just as they are, and a place to be personal about the simple aches and joys of life they experience in trying to live for Christ—subjects which many of them cannot discuss in their marriages. People become open and really love each other.

Although nothing may be said about sex, this can be a very sexual situation, in a broader sense than that of which I have been speaking. The kind of openness and acceptance among Christians is that which everyone longs for in marriage, and which in marriage would naturally lead to a complete giving of ourselves to each other. But Christ is the center of Christian groups. And the knowledge that he has saved us from despair and from ourselves helps us to appreciate as brothers and sisters this wonderful gift of spiritual closeness. Because of a common commitment to Christ and the finding of his will, this acceptance of each other is usually just a wonderful and creative experience.

When I began to accept the love of God and find the freedom to open my life to other people, particularly to Christians in a small group, I began to see that in the loving Christian fellowship we are dealing with some very powerful and basic human needs. Most of us in our generation are so starved for any kind of love and

---

* Although this is not the place to discuss in detail the tragic sexual drifting apart which so often takes place in Christian marriages after a few years because of breakdown in communication, I think Reuel Howe has done an excellent job of discussing this delicate subject in *The Creative Years* (New York: Seabury Press, 1965).

Christian Sexuality / 163

true acceptance that when we open our lives to God and to our fellow Christians, we may find ourselves at some time thinking of the bedroom instead of the upper room. And this can be a real surprise when you think your motives are purely spiritual.

What does an active lay person do to avoid this sort of problem? In talking this matter over with some very perceptive Christians, I have come to believe that a deep understanding of the weakness of the human will is a good start. But in talking to lay people about counseling as Christians, I have found a couple of practical suggestions helpful with regard to relations between men and women:

(1) Any time a man or woman sets up a *continuing* relationship with a member of the opposite sex in an unstructured situation in which they are together privately, the chances of some kind of sexual involvement not taking place would appear to be small. And the fact that the content of the discussion is "Christianity" or "prayer," seems to make almost no difference. As a matter of fact, there may be a broader truth in the old cliché, "Couples who pray together, stay together," than is generally recognized.

(2) For nonprofessional counseling over a period of time, I have found it better for men to counsel with men and women with women. A Christian lay Sunday school teacher or small-group leader who finds himself doing a lot of counseling can usually find a perceptive Christian woman to whom he can refer women counselees—particularly those who want to have someone with whom to pray and discuss personal problems over a period of time.

(3) Since a lot of the new lay counseling goes on at conferences in resort-type settings, it seems wise to avoid counseling someone of the opposite sex privately in a hotel room. This advice may seem overly cautious, but any type of intimate meeting alone to talk about loneliness and problems in marriage can be a considerable strain on nonpresent spouses—not to mention latent gamesmanship between the sexes.

Many of you may think I am either overly pious or a lecherous ogre for taking the time to deal with such a seemingly outlandish problem. But because of the tragedies in the lives of some strong and dedicated Christian families, and the unfortunate degeneration of some small-group experiments of the past, I am taking the risk of discussing these problems.

Some Christians may react to this discussion with, "Well, if there is a chance for anything like *that* happening, let's don't get mixed up in small groups." But that would be a tragic attitude to take. In the first place the strength and companionship of a Christian fellowship have kept many people from the desperation of trading their bodies for some personal love and attention. Besides, any time there is real life and healing going on, there are dangers of excesses. Look at any of the reformations of the past.

One of my friends, whom I respect tremendously, suggested that I delete this section, because "people are just looking for a way to discredit lay renewal." But I think the time has come to face openly both the problems and the joys of the Christian life. At least, those who commit themselves to Christ now will not be with a bunch of people who are afraid to face the dangers as well as the opportunities of real living. I personally believe our generation is looking for this open attitude instead of that which has so often prevailed in the church of, "Oh, we must not talk about that or they will think . . ." If anyone thinks these sorts of problems are new in the Christian community, ask him to check Paul's letters to the earliest Christian small groups (e.g., 1 Cor. 5:1 f.).

"How does a deeply committed Christian face the problem of sexual lust?"

Ever since I was a young boy in high school I have liked girls. This disposition has brought a good bit of conflict as well as happiness into my experience. At the time I became a Christian, Mary Allen and I loved each other and had a marriage which seemed very good to us, a marriage which we were both trying to make better. I wasn't committing adultery, and we were very much in love, so I thought this was one area in which I would not have immediate problems as a Christian. But in discussions, by the silence I encountered, I began to get the idea that for many Christians sex is an evil area of life. Because of this, I began to be more conscious of committing those casual, fleeting "walking down the street" adulteries in my imagination. These little scenarios were so natural I had not even thought of them as adulteries, until I read what Christ said: "If a man looks on a woman with a lustful eye, he has already committed adultery with her in his heart" (Matt. 5:28).* That statement, if true, gave adultery a real home in my inner life.

At first I was horrified. I said to myself, "Man, if giving up

---

* In the context in which this passage is set, I think Jesus was trying to tell his listeners that purity from God's perspective was something they could not even understand in terms of their legalistic viewpoint. The kind of goodness which is demanded by God in terms of perfection none of them had.

Christian Sexuality / 165

noticing good-looking women is a prerequisite for getting into heaven, I know three things: (1) I'll never make it; (2) there's no need for me to witness to my friends because they would never make it either, and (3) what kind of men will there be in heaven with whom I could identify for an eternity?"

But as I began to look more closely at the dynamics of this almost universal experience of noticing, as a reflex action, the potential sexual compatibility of a member of the opposite sex, I began to realize what I had done. I had identified the instant (and automatic) recognition I have just described with the subsequent imaginary episode of committing adultery with the person noticed.

I have found that becoming a deeply committed Christian does not keep one from being fully aware of beauty in the opposite sex. And I do not think this recognition is in any sense sin or is an indication that one needs a spiritual checkup. In fact, if you do not recognize physical beauty in the opposite sex, and if you are my age, you may need a physical checkup. I am very serious. "Recognition" in my opinion is never sin. As a matter of fact, recognition of specific possibility for sinning is a prerequisite for the development of Christian character. For instance, no blind man would be considered honest for not stealing a gold coin on a table before him—only a man who saw the gold piece and recognized fully his drive for it but chose not to steal it. Besides, if temptation is sin, then Christ was not sinless, for he was tempted (see Luke 4:1–13). It is what one *does* with what is recognized that causes the problems.

Over six hundred years ago, Thomas à Kempis discussed the process of succumbing to temptation with great clarity. He de-

---

And Christ began to cut the ground from under their pitiful legalistic type of righteousness. He told them their goodness would have to be far greater than that of the scribes and Pharisees before they could set foot in the Kingdom of heaven. For instance, he told them, true purity involves the inner as well as the outer expression of the desires, and he listed inner adultery, inner hate, etc., and caught them all.

Fortunately, with this delineation of godly perfection comes the news that we are saved by grace through faith (Eph. 2:8). But I think Christians should understand clearly that Christianity historically has taken a definite stand against adultery and filling one's imagination with fantasies of adultery. It is amazing what regular church attendance and a pious mask can cover up in a deacon's or vestryman's—or a minister's—inner life (or that of their spouses).

scribed the coming into the mind of an evil thought, followed by a strong elaborating of the thought as it is led by the thinker into the inner chamber of the imagination; "then a sense of delight; then a perverse impulse and assenting." He points out that the only practical place to stop temptation is at the point of seeing or recognizing, "for the enemy is more easily overcome if he is refused entrance to the door of the mind, and resisted on the threshold at the first knock." [3] After the first assenting and turning the situation over to the imagination, the outcome seems to be pretty well decided. So the only place one may be able to stop the process is at the point of recognition.

I realize that all of this may seem strange material to be included in a book about trying to live the adventure of faith. But I have listened to some apparently sophisticated Christian people who are guilt-ridden inside over these and other very common personal issues which were "hidden" from the fellowship of Christians. And having wondered alone about so many things, we are just getting a few out in the open so that you can consider them. Because of the constant exposure to sexually attractive people on TV, in magazines, and on the street, there is no way to hide as a Christian, even if you choose to. But if you really become concerned with the amount of your attention which is absorbed by lust, you can change the activity in your imagination to an amazing degree by varying your selection of books, magazines, and movies. As Martin Luther put it a good many years ago, "You cannot keep the birds from flying over your head, but you can keep them from nesting in your hair."

Chapter Nine

Christian Community and Uniqueness

MEMORANDUM

TO: Bruce
FROM: Keith
RE: Chapter Nine—Christian Community and Uniqueness

Dear Bruce:

Boy, this is one nobody's solved! Almost all the experiments in community I know have been either short-lived or shallow. I believe there are some paradoxes in thinking about community and uniqueness. People seem to think that "community" refers to a large group of worshipers and "uniqueness" refers to loners and solo renegades.

How about putting something in here concerning what you think God helps each person to find and bring to community? After we begin getting a glimpse of who we are, how does our sense of uniqueness affect our relationships? And, finally, what are the elements which combine to help us discover community as Christians?

Keith

Finding Your True Name

It seems that I never lose my childlike sense of anticipation for what the daily mail might bring. Usually it's bills or bulk mail or endless printed things. But on the good days I find a letter from an old friend, from one of our kids away at school, or a letter of appreciation from someone who is reading one of my books.

One of those welcomed letters came recently from a minister in Grand Rapids, Michigan. We had never met, but it seems that while he was reading *Ask Me to Dance,* his seventeen-year-old son was killed in an automobile accident. This new friend went on to tell me how the book had been a needed reminder for him and his wife of God's love and resources in this time of grief. He enclosed a copy of a letter he had written to his son on the day that he was born which was to be opened on the boy's eighteenth birthday—the birthday they would now never celebrate.

The letter tells this new little boy of his parents' feelings as they anticipated his arrival and of their excitement about his birth. It goes on to speak of their hopes and dreams for his future and ends with these two wonderful paragraphs:

> There are so many things that I should like to say to you today, bits of advice and words of suggestion for the life that awaits you. Suffice it all to say that you and your mother have made me the happiest man on earth. I have literally been walking on air! Even forgot early this morning when in Paynesville on business that parking meters had a purpose until I saw a motorcycle cop coming down the street. That fine of one dollar, my son, is your first cost to me! I laughed like mad and surrendered the dollar willingly to the court. For you were worth more than a buck to me, you were worth a million and then some!
>
> And now, you and I will be entering into a father-son relationship! Difficult sometimes, to say the least. I, too, had a father; and I know that I was a rascal on more than one occasion—and knowing that you will be a "chip off the old

block," I predict the same for you. And on the other hand, sometimes, I'll be a bit overbearing and somewhat of a problem to you; but do please bear with me. I know how wonderful your mother is—she'll be a referee deluxe and ever do her best to make our home always "home, sweet home." No matter what comes in the course of the years, may this passage from the parable of the prodigal son, where the father speaks to his elder son, ever govern and guide and guard that relationship between us. "My son, you and I are always together" (Luke 15:31). "Always together" in life and death, let us be.

I was deeply touched by this father's letter written seventeen years before, and I wish that I had had the foresight to write such a letter to each of my own three children when they were born. It can be a priceless gift. In fact, I have a similar letter written to me by my father the day before he died. I was eighteen and in the army during World War II. He was in St. Luke's Hospital in Chicago facing surgery. He wrote telling something of his dreams for me and of what he hoped we could do and be together when the war was over.

I still have and treasure my father's letter. Somehow it was a key to who I was at a time when I wasn't certain about much of anything. Before I found God, it represented my firmest grip on the mystery of my own identity. Somehow I was the person my father told me I was. Erik Erikson, the great psychoanalyst and self-educated philosopher, has given us the term "identity-crisis." But long before Erikson, man has known that the great quest was his own search for identity. The man of faith knows that his search for himself is inextricably bound up with his search for God.

Your Name and God's Letter to You

I believe the biblical revelation of God is in essence the fact that God knows your name. And at the very moment of your birth, and even before, when you were only a thought in your father's mind or a seed in your mother's womb, God knew your name and wrote you a letter. In part he says, "John (Jane), there is nobody else like you. Nobody with your genes. Nobody with your past or potential experience. Nobody who will have your parents, your friends, or your influences. You are the one and only you that I made and I want to tell you who you are." Your letter from God is like the one he wrote to Jeremiah. "Before I formed you in the womb I knew you" (Jer. 1:5). But it is tragic that so many people never read the letter God wrote to them before they were born. They are like my new friend's son who died before reading the beautiful and moving letter that his father wrote.

It is in finding the letter God wrote to you and to no one else that you find yourself in all of your unique and mysterious personality. The problem of so many people today can be summed up in the phrase, "I am a wandering generality." I believe it is possible for a person to find God and still not find himself. But I do not believe that you can find yourself truly without finding God.

The message of hope that we have is that God loves us and knows our names. He has written you a letter, and faith is trusting God enough to let him show you this letter. The Bible corroborates this again and again. Jacob had his life changed while wrestling with the angel at the brook Jabbok. There God gave him a new name, "Israel," which means prince. From that moment on Jacob was a new man (Gen. 32:22–32). At the scene of the burning bush God called Moses by name, and his life was radically changed as he was called to new leadership (Exod. 3–4). And today, God calls *you* by *your* name to demonstrate that he is, in fact, God. Hearing someone whose very inflections indicate that he knows you indicates that the one who calls you is not man, but God himself.

Samuel, who became a great prophet, first encountered God directly when he heard his own name in the dark of night. God called repeatedly, "Samuel, Samuel." The old priest Eli finally understood who was calling and instructed the boy to respond the next time he heard his name by saying, "Speak, thy servant hears thee" (1 Sam. 3).

When the Apostle Paul met the risen Christ on the Damascus Road, the first thing he heard was his own name: "Saul, Saul, why do you persecute me?" (Acts 9:1–9). Over and over again the authenticating mark of God speaking to us is that he uses our name or gives us a new name or speaks to us as the One who knows us and holds the key to our identity. And so, finding God is coming home.

The Hospitality of Genuine Community

The newspaperman Robert G. Kaiser tells about an American

who vacationed in Tbilisi a short while ago. A friend in New York had suggested that while he was there he might look up a certain Russian journalist from the province of Georgia. Installed in his hotel, the American called the journalist. "What are you doing tonight?" the Georgian asked. "Nothing," responded the American. "Stay right there. We'll pick you up in half an hour." The journalist and his wife drove the American and his companion to a restaurant in the hills outside of Tbilisi and ordered a traditional Georgian banquet. Hours later, as they finished the last of many courses and prepared to leave the restaurant, the Georgian turned to his American guest, "I didn't understand you on the telephone. Who did you say gave you my name?"

Mr. Kaiser insists that is a true story. At any rate, I would like to think so, because for me it is a parable of what it is like to meet God. If you think Georgians are notorious for their hospitality —try God's! The prodigal son coming home doesn't have to tell about all the humiliation, the failures, and the hurts of the far country. He doesn't even have to promise he'll stay home and be good. He finds a loving welcome from someone who is glad to see him and who asks no questions.

Your Uniqueness

At every level of a person's life there seems to be universal conspiracy of conformity. It doesn't matter whether you are religious, educated, or illiterate, a rebel or a conformist. There is an innate desire in all of us to conform, if only to a handful of other rebels or to a nonconformist from a prior age (a St. Francis or Thoreau).

Now if God made each person to be unique, a one-and-only version of that life, then sin can be expressed when internal and external forces cause us to lose our uniqueness and become a carbon copy—and usually a poor one—of another person or group. So the change that God offers is one that helps a person to find his true identity, his true personhood.

In studying the factors in personality development and human behavior, two very different trends have emerged in psychology. Sigmund Freud is the father of one: depth psychology. The premise of depth psychology is that deep in the unconscious all people are alike. When you peel off layer after layer of all the things that have accrued in our personalities, we are all motivated by sex, aggression, and fear. Simply put, if we go deep enough, all people are basically the same.

But another school of psychology has emerged—trait psychology—of which Gordon Allport is the acknowledged founder. In trait psychology and its many branches, psychologists are saying that since all people are alike at their deepest levels, it is the surface traits that are really important in determining who a person is. It is in the areas where people are different that we find personality and individuality emerging.

It seems to me that each of these schools of psychology has part of a vital truth. We cannot choose one or the other as the whole explanation of human personality. If we adopt the premise of depth psychology exclusively and assume that everyone else is just like us, then we begin to project on people around us our own feelings, our own hopes, our own fears. I tend to turn other people off because, having met myself, I think I've met everyone and no one else is really worth meeting. I find myself finishing people's stories because I know how they will end. I become more and more cut off and lonely because I have everyone all figured out. Instead of listening to people, I give advice.

If, on the other hand, I only emphasize all those traits that make me different, I may begin to feel that "I am unique. There is no one else like me." Operating on that premise I begin to feel superior or be guarded. I can't let people know who I am because of my peculiarities. I cut myself off from all possibilities of love and relationship, of belonging and being. And the result is disastrous!

The Christian ideal may be a community in which one can discover both his unique traits and his common depths in the Body of Christ.

Discovering Community

In fact, one of the great priorities of the church in our time is to help people discover community.

But it is elusive. Perhaps this is because we are uncertain of the ingredients necessary to create community. A recent experience helped me enormously to understand what some of those ingredients might be. I was part of the faculty for a seminar for church leaders who were going to spend two weeks cruising the Caribbean visiting mission stations and studying relational theology. We had been told in advance that buses would be waiting at the airport in Miami to take us directly to our ship. I boarded a bus in which there were possibly a dozen people all heading for the *Starward*. What we didn't realize, as we started off, was that because of a bus drivers' strike, we had a scab driver.

That bothered some of us who are sensitive about the church's witness in labor relations. But it bothered all of us when we learned that our driver did not know the way to the ship. He got hopelessly lost, took us dozens of miles out of our way, and stopped frequently to radio headquarters to find out where he was and where he should go. As the hour drew near for departure, we became increasingly nervous and fearful. But the amazing thing is that somehow this made us a very tight-knit, loving, and supportive community. In fact, those of us who shared that crazy bus ride had something special going for us during the remaining two weeks on the boat.

What were the ingredients of that bus trip? Well, as I've analyzed it, there were six—all essential to genuine community. First of all, there was adventure, and most of us respond positively to adventure. Shared adventure builds fellowship. Next, there was worry and fear at various levels which were openly communicated. When people are worried and fearful together, a kind of mutual dependency is created. Third, we had a common problem. We were all lost. A common problem inspires a sense of fellowship. Fourth, we had a need for each other. We gave encouragement and support to each other. Fifth, we had a great sense of fun. This experience had probably never happened to any of us before and would never happen again, and we were involved in something that would never be forgotten. Sixth, our leader had the grace not to pretend that he knew how to get where we were going—he was honest about being lost and involved us in the whole process. We were participating with him in searching for a solution.

I think this says a good deal about the kind of community the church is striving for and the role of the clergy and lay leaders in that community. They are the drivers of our ecclesiastical bus, and they need to let us know when they are lost so that together we can share the adventure and participate in the whole fearful and exhilarating prospect of being the people of God on mission.

On fall days I always watch for those marvelous overhead dramas when Canadian geese fly in V-formation. As I understand it, there is not one lead goose. Rather, specialists in aero-

Christian Community and Uniqueness / 175

dynamics say that geese can fly so far and so long because each one helps the flock by taking his turn as leader.

In a wind tunnel, two engineers discovered what happens to the formation of geese. Each goose in flapping its own wings creates an upward lift for the following goose. This gives the whole flock seventy-one percent greater flying range than if each bird flew alone. Leadership is rotated because no goose can stay up there very long. If an individual goose falls back and begins to think, "Nobody will miss me in this crowd," he immediately feels the heavier load of flying alone and speeds up to get back into the formation. Bird fanciers seem to feel that those who fall behind are encouraged by the honking of their peers.

There is a significant application here for us in the area of community. We can't stay way out in front alone for very long. But together, if we rotate leadership and begin to build on each other's weaknesses and help one another, we can extend the range and the scope of our spiritual adventure.

MEMORANDUM

TO: Keith

FROM: Bruce

RE: Chapter Nine—Christian Community and Uniqueness

Dear Keith:

I've discussed the questions you suggested and some others. But in thinking about the subject of community, I remember reading several things you've written about trying to **experience** community in small groups.

Why don't you take us through the process you tried? How did you begin? And how do you think the Christian community looks at creative uniqueness? I suppose that leads to the question: how do you think community and uniqueness are related?

Bruce

Christian Community

One of the most puzzling problems a new Christian faces as he comes into the church and begins to read the Bible is that there is so much *written* and *said* about a loving community or family in Christ, and yet no place to *experience* such a community. People smile and "extend the right hand of fellowship." But the actual sharing of inner journeys is often almost nonexistent in large Christian congregations—even many which are known for their "spirituality" or their giving of time and money to social concerns.

When I had made a beginning commitment and started becoming involved in the church's program, I taught an adult class on Sunday mornings that brought me in weekly contact with over a hundred people. But *we did not really know each other* or anything about sharing our Christian journeys. I didn't realize this personally for some months. *I* was feeling known and accepted because I was revealing *myself* to *them* in small bits through my lessons. So I was experiencing some sense of belonging in the community. I sometimes wonder if many ministers don't fall into that same trap—thinking there is community in their churches because *they* speak in the pulpit and are accepted—but not realizing almost no one else has a place to be known and loved.

The people in the Sunday school class seemed to accept me and believe what I told them. But their lives were not changing—at least they were not changing in any way I could see. And I was lonely for some personal contact with other strugglers.

A Beginning Experiment

Out of my own loneliness and discouragement I decided to ask a few people to begin meeting with me one night a week for an eight weeks' trial period. My first inclination was to ask some of the "other" leaders of the church, my thinking being that if they would see this new life, the whole town might come alive. But they were almost all too busy with meetings, etc., to want to come.

So I thought about Christ and what he did. Then I decided that I would look around the church and find eleven or twelve people who seemed most hungry to know God, whoever they might be.

I found a couple who were dear friends who had just lost a child, a divorcee, a young man getting ready to go to seminary, a couple who had no children, a woman who had come into the Episcopal church from the Roman Catholic church recently, a man who sold heavy road equipment, and one couple in the building business with four children. I went to see these people individually and told them what was happening in my life. I asked them if they would like to meet with other people who were seeking to know Christ. The only criterion for joining the group was that each of the people had to want to give his life to God (even though he might not be able to do it).

We decided that the clear purpose was to be getting to know the living Christ and each other—and how to live together for him. We also decided to make an experiment with each one of our lives during that period. We reported back to the group each week concerning our failures, our joys, and the ridiculous things which happened to us as we tried to take Christ consciously through the routine of our days and nights. We made it sort of a secretive thing . . . like an underground experiment. And we came back to each meeting with an excitement as we began to see how strangely timid and insecure we were in our faith. We could laugh at ourselves and vicariously experience through each other the fears and joys and insights of a life with Christ in the center of it.

Three-Part Meeting

We divided the time into three sections during those evenings. As we shared the problems and discoveries of that week during the first part of the evening, we began to see together the fresh and contemporary footprints of Christ through our lives. We studied the Bible. Most of the people never really had and admitted that they were ashamed of how little they knew about the content of the Bible. And we spent the last part of the evening praying together.

As those eight weeks grew into two years, and as we studied the Bible and shared our own real questions, we found that we had never really known each other at all before the group started. We discovered that we had not been able to communicate because we were basically afraid of each other somehow and did not know how to reveal our true thoughts, questions, and opinions without being embarrassed.

Over the next two years all of us found new life in our own church experience. Now that we had something to talk about and we had a personal place in a "family" within the church, Christ was not a distant figure but through the Holy Spirit he was becoming alive in our midst. We felt a different kind of love for each other, for other people, and for him. We got involved in the church's work in things like tithing and teaching, as by-products of our life together. And I saw that community itself may be a by-product of the kind of common search we were on.

Leadership in Christian Community

My whole concept of leadership in community took a sudden change. I can remember the strange paradox as "leader" when the group finally came alive. In the beginning Mary Allen had been skeptical about having a regular gathering of people with different backgrounds in terms of age, marital status, social habits, and interests and hoping for any kind of common ground. But I felt that these were the people whom God had given us. And besides, if it failed nothing would be hurt but my pride. I wasn't selling anything; so we tried it.

Things went pretty smoothly until about the third meeting. To put us all on a more equal basis and to force us to examine the Scriptures for ourselves, no one, including the leader, was allowed to use the Bible commentaries until *after* the session in which a passage was discussed. This saved the people from the anxiety of expressing an honest opinion for fear the leader had *the* answer and was ready to pounce on them with it.

But about the third meeting, I expressed an opinion about the meaning of the passage, and two of the members of the group disagreed heartily. A third took up their position. We checked the passage for study in the secondary sources for the next week, and the meeting ended. As it turned out they were right and I was wrong. I felt sick. I had been so sure that I was right. I felt that I had failed them as a leader and that they would lose confidence in me and the group would disintegrate. I told all this to Mary Allen and was reconciled to my failure. But during that week one member of the group after another called, filled with enthusiasm, telling me they thought that at last we were "getting together" somehow and that that meeting had meant more to them than any of the others.

Right then two thoughts struck me. The first was that a Christian leader in a forming community must die in a sense to his own image of perfection that others may live. Now the people realized I was just one of them and that they too were first-class citizens and not just "my group." My being wrong and their being able to help me did something for all of us. I quit feeling pressured to be right all of the time as leader and relaxed (at least some of the time I relaxed). They gained a new kind of group confidence and freedom.

Second, it hit me that when the leader is in control and things "feel good" to him about a meeting, it is not necessarily good from the *participants'* perspective. Many times the leader's very painful experience of "laying down his life for his friends" in witnessing to his own failure and being vulnerable makes for an exciting and joyous breakthrough for the rest of the group. This seeing *them* come alive and gain confidence was paradoxically a greater joy than having a "successful group" as a smooth leader. This was true even though my pride seemed to be taking all kinds of blows which were agonizing for me.

Community: People not Meetings

As the months had gone by and we had met in each other's homes to pray and talk about Jesus Christ, our homes became more natural places to talk about him during other nights of the week. And we discovered that Christian community does not take place in a particular context or building but is caring people going into all kinds of places and contexts. We began to learn vicariously through each other's experiences away from the group. And out of this sharing concrete suggestions often came which we might not have stumbled onto alone for years because of our lack of perspective, each being too close to his own problems.

As we began to taste community and to feel at home with others, some of us began seeing that we were more accepted when we were our unique selves. We saw that the freedom to be ourselves in the group encouraged us to live more naturally everywhere we went.

Christian Community and Uniqueness / 181

We were discovering the generally unrecognized paradox that genuine Christian community is a seedbed for the discovery and development of the *creative uniqueness of the individual members.*

Christian Uniqueness—the Battle against an Unreal Conformity

Creative uniqueness is not generally encouraged in most churches with which I am familiar. As a matter of fact, young Christians are often told either implicitly or explicitly that they should be like the other good members. They should "be consistent" in their habits and relationships, rather than creatively unique in their responses to life. Uniqueness seems to carry a faint implication of heresy.

I was ill. Because the more I was living in what I thought was Christ's perspective on this adventure of faith, in one sense the more inconsistent my behavior seemed to be—according to some teaching around the church about how to live and witness. Being very insecure I would go back and try to conform.

Jesus Was Inconsistent?

I was pretty discouraged and confused. But then I saw a surprising thing in reading the New Testament. Whereas I had always blindly assumed that Christ was very consistent in his life, I saw suddenly that he was not. In fact, Jesus was very inconsistent in his life! And it was his inconsistency, according to the religious habits of his day, which kept him in hot water and eventually led to his death. For example, on one hand he said that he had not come to change even the smallest punctuation mark of the Jewish law (Matt. 5:17 f.). Then he proceeded to break their sacred rules one after the other—even on the Sabbath—to love the people from his Father's perspective in obedience to him (Mark 2:15–17, 18–22, 23–28; 3:1–5). He told his followers not to use physical violence to conquer the world. In fact, he told them that they should turn the other cheek (Matt. 5:39). But in a later situation we see a furious Jesus, driving employees out of the Temple and knocking over their stalls (Matt. 21:12). Or on another occasion we see him telling a group of scribes and Pharisees that they were so rotten inside that from his perspective they had internal B.O. (Matt. 23:27–28). Then a few days or weeks later, he died for them. These are just a few of the acts of a Man who was notoriously inconsistent. Why did he behave that way?

I realized that in my insecurity, I had unconsciously assumed that consistency in Christian living meant uniformity—that we were all supposed to act alike and to respond the same way all the time. I guess I had assumed that what God is doing is recruiting a sort of "spiritual trumpet corps," each member like the next one ethically and morally. And in order to be consistent with our own group, we begin to take on a conformity to its "sound." We witness and pray alike. We see at which angle we are to hold the trumpet and when we are to pick it up and put it down.

I believe that I can listen to a man either preach or pray and tell you (a good many times out of ten) in what denomination he was trained or even the interdenominational group through which he got converted—by the sound of his language, which is usually unconscious to him. Baptists have a different "sound" from Presbyterians, for instance; they use different names for God when they pray, etc. The academic theologians and social action groups each have their own pet phrases and identifying words, their own sounds.

In my unconscious desire for consistency with our group, I think I have tuned out some people who might really have helped me to wholeness in Christ. At least I let an artificial barrier separate me from part of Christ's Body.

But the new discovery to me is that the Christian church is not a trumpet corps—but an orchestra. We are not all supposed to sound alike because each of us is a different-shaped instrument. God has given us our own individual sounds, our own unique lives. For years I have been a piccolo trying to play in the tuba section, because some men I admire greatly play the spiritual "deep notes." Can you imagine anything more pitiful than a piccolo trying to play in the tuba section? Yet this is the story of much of my life. I had never felt free and natural in my Christian living because I had always tried to be something I was not, so that I could be "like a child of God" (like those other children of God around me).

Jesus' Kind of Consistency

Where, then, had this idea come from that Jesus lived a consistent life and, therefore, we ought to also? Then I knew. Jesus was not consistent with regard to a set of rules.* He lived out his days in consistent obedience to a living creative Composer, who was composing a masterpiece of lives and giving Jesus his part in it to play a line, an hour at a time, as he listened and watched in his life. To be obedient to the perspective of his Father in new situations, Jesus transcended the old rules. He tried to bring God's vulnerable but healing love to each situation in a way that brought wholeness to the people involved, however inconsistent his behavior might seem to the secular mind or even to the Jewish keepers of the truth and defenders of the faith.

Uniqueness and Community

Some religious leaders have always thought people who talk about this kind of call to uniqueness are talking about a kind of irresponsible license, a kind of renegade freedom from discipline and responsibility to other members of Christ's Body. But, of course, this is not true. As a matter of fact, I am finding that trying to discover and live creatively in Christ's perspective is far more demanding in terms of prayer, study of the Scriptures, corporate worship, and listening to God and to other struggling Christians, than it was to follow the standard rules outlined by our part of the Christian community. It is the practice of these disciplines in community which, in fact, acts as a valuable check against a rootless subjectivism as one is discovering the unique shape of his own life.

What this says to me is that an authentic Christian who is becoming that person he was most nearly "designed" to be in community does not wind up being an imitator when he becomes mature. Of course, at first we must imitate other Christians as Paul suggested (Phil. 3:17). We have to pick up the openness and life-style of the Christian family way in the company of the committed. But as a person becomes more devoted to Christ and more transparent in being who he is, he does less posturing and imitating. This might mean, for instance, that the more totally and transparently I am being Keith Miller with you, living for God, the more nearly you will see Jesus Christ through me. And

---
* I am not talking about the Ten Commandments, which Jesus did obey of course. But with regard to men's relationships he and Paul both tried to summarize all these laws into a *perspective of love* to avoid the kind of legalism of which I am speaking (Matt. 22:37 f., Rom. 13:9 f.).

although the Scriptures indicate that we all receive the same Spirit and are to imitate God in being loving, each of us will be given the grace and the specific gifts we particularly need to grow up in Christ's perspective (see Eph. 4).

If this is true, then God is not making imitations of anything—even Jesus. He is creating authentic, unique human beings who have the sound of Love in their lives and who unconsciously leave the fragrance of Christ behind them wherever they go.

Chapter Ten

Christian "Success"

MEMORANDUM

TO: Bruce
FROM: Keith
RE: Chapter Ten—Christian "Success"

Dear Bruce:

I've been so success-oriented all my life that "failure" and being caught in stupid mistakes have furnished lots of material for bad dreams at night and motivation for great efforts to succeed in the daytime. I bet there are a good many other people who don't understand "success" and its motivating force in their lives.

Why don't you talk about what being a success means to you. Is success different for a Christian than for anyone else? How do you check your priorities to determine your true values? What happens when we try to hide what we are? And how do you begin letting God change you toward being his type of "success"?

Keith

What Is "Success"?

Someone once said, "Behind every successful man there is a very surprised mother-in-law." That may be true. But a more important issue is, "What is in front of any successful person?"

In other words, what does success mean to the person? How does one set for himself goals that are authentic and satisfying and then go about obtaining those goals?

I remember an old friend of the family who retired in his early sixties with all the money he would ever need. He was a heavy drinker and a chain-smoker and his doctor warned him that unless he stopped both habits he would be dead within six months. With more temperate living, he was told, he could possibly live for many years. Without hesitation, he replied: "Doctor, I'd rather live one day drinking and smoking than ten years without."

Well, the prediction was accurate and he was dead in less than six months. I question the values that led to this man's choice, but I must say that I have always been impressed with his knowing what was important to him.

What are the things that represent success for you? Psychologists tell us the primary goal for most of us in the Western world is to control people and our environment, while the primary cultural goal for Orientals is simply to fit in. What is your summum bonum, your highest value, your ultimate goal? What is that one thing for which you would trade all else? Money? Health? Power? Friends? Wisdom? Fame? A clear conscience? A record of helping others? Some tangible contribution to mankind? Inner peace? Integration? Self-acceptance? Transcendence? Subjugation of the flesh?

"Getting" Something or "Being" Something

It seems to me that any of the possible answers we might give to this question, "What is success?" would necessarily fall into one of two categories. Basically, success is either getting something or being something.

Pogo, the famous cartoon possum, says, "We have met the enemy, and they is us!"

This is the message stamped upon the literature of the Western world. But, if our goals have to do with acquiring things, including fame, wealth, and position, then the enemy is always *other people*. They stand in our way or keep us from what we want or block us in some way. On the other hand, if being or becoming something is your idea of success then, of course, the enemy is always within. It is helpful in my own personal quest for success to know whether I've got to overcome others or conquer myself.

Two Gospels

I had been thinking about this whole matter for some time, when my thoughts culminated one night in a dream. I saw two different men living in the same town. One man grew up as the blessed child of his parents, the envy of his brothers and sisters, the captain of his team, the president of his class, and one who walked with ease and grace among his peers. He learned early in life how to get what he wanted from people and how to use them for his own purposes. Eventually he became the head of a prospering business, with a wife of his choosing, a house full of healthy children, two cars in the garage, honors, medals, fame, and all the rest.

One day he went into a little chapel and heard someone speak about a Christ who could make one a participant in the whole business of love. He heard for the first time about losing one's life for Christ, of taking up one's cross, of laying down one's life for others, of taking up a towel and a basin. He returned to his family and friends as a transformed man. Freed of the need to dominate and manipulate people, he saw that Christ could make him a servant of others. So he began to be sensitive to the needs of his wife, his children, his staff, and his friends. He entered into a whole new life of servanthood and subsequently found the joy, peace, and fulfillment that had eluded him. He became a blessing to countless people.

In time this man began to teach the adult Bible class and eventually left his business and became a preacher. He never ceased to preach about a Christ who called people to submit their lives to him and to lose their lives in service to others.

Now in this same town there was another man. The middle

child of a large family, he was neglected by his mother and father. He had no sense of worth and no real identity. He never excelled in sports or academics and never held a class office. He married the first girl who'd have him, sure he'd never get a second chance. He stayed with the first company that hired him and never got very far up the organizational ladder. His life was gray and dull and meaningless until one day he happened into a little chapel and heard someone preaching about Christ as the source, center and giver of life. The gospel he heard emphasized becoming sons of God, having a crown in heaven, judging the universe, being lord of the angels, having the hairs of your head numbered, and being of infinite worth.

This man began to believe he was somebody because of Jesus Christ. He came home and began to assert himself with his wife. He began to guide strongly and firmly in the lives of his children. His new quality of leadership at the office began to pay off with raises and greater responsibilities. This man, too, was asked to teach a class in his church and ultimately, because so many responded to him and to his preaching, he too entered the ministry. His gospel proclaimed that a man can do all things through Christ who lives in him. He can achieve, he can start movements and build empires.

So now we find these two born-again, Spirit-filled men attracting others. One has started a church of Dynamic Doormatism, while the other leads a church of the Holy Achievers. Each man is preaching Christ and each out of his own experience of Christ. But one is calling men to lose their lives and to serve others. The other is calling men to begin to be a somebody and to achieve great things for Christ. Each man is sincere and authentic. Each man is a "success."

Is Salvation Success for the Christian?

For Christians, an important question is whether or not "success" can be equated with salvation. If being or becoming means most to me, then, as a Christian, Jesus is the means and the way by which I obtain this goal, and essentially success and salvation are indistinguishable.

I'm writing this at the famous Menninger Foundation in Topeka, Kansas, where I am spending a week. I am studying many of the training techniques that have made this a pioneer center in exploring the interrelatedness of the medical, social, spiritual, and psychological disciplines. A quote heard often here is from David Neiswanger, "If each of us can be helped by science to live a hundred years, what will it profit us if our hates and fears, our loneliness and our remorse will not permit us to enjoy them? What use is an extra year or two to the man who 'kills' what time he has?"

This profound question needs to be answered honestly in the private soul of every human being. Of course it's nothing more nor less than a secular and medical paraphrase of what Jesus said originally: "What will a man gain by winning the whole world, at the cost of his true self?" (Matt. 16:27). You can succeed in attaining a lesser goal and still miss your number one goal. If you attain your goal—life, health, money, power, or wisdom—only to find that there is something else more important you want, then you have gained what for you is the world, but have lost what for you is your self—your ultimate value.

Some Traits of Wholeness

If success and salvation are closely allied, we need to remember that *salvation* really means wholeness. Therefore, wholeness of body, mind, and spirit is a legitimate goal. In a research project done recently at the Menninger Foundation, twelve senior clinicians were asked to think of the six or eight patients that they had seen in their lifetime who had exhibited the best mental health and to list some of their traits and qualities. Of the eighty to a hundred patients described, all of them had five traits in common.

1. An enjoyment of what they were doing. (They were active and productive in work that was rewarding and meaningful.)
2. The ability to treat others as individuals and not as stereotypes.
3. Flexibility under stress.
4. The ability to recognize and accept their own assets and liabilities.
5. A wide variety of sources of gratification. (A doctor teaching one of the courses in my seminar explained that he advises people to "diversify your psychological investment portfolio." I like that!)

These five marks of mental health will usually accompany any genuine success. If the goal I have reached does not produce these as a by-product, then I would suspect that I have not, in fact, found success—whether I am a Christian or not.

Checking Priorities

Last December I sat in the Hollywood Presbyterian Church and listened to my longtime friend, Lloyd Ogilvie, preach. It was a sermon meant just for me. Lloyd was sharing some of his own struggles in preparing the sermon for that day. As he sat in his study one night trying to sort out the priorities of his life, he asked himself what things were not negotiable. What things would he or could he not do without. Because, you see, if one knows what he *cannot* do without, then he will know all the things he *can* do without.

As I went back to the hotel room that afternoon with my wife Hazel, I found that the sermon prompted a similar search in me. Finally, I realized that the only thing I had to have was the knowledge that I was loved and accepted by God and Jesus Christ as I am. With that knowledge I could take any vicissitude, pressure, or loss that life might give. I enjoy health. I enjoy having enough to take care of my family and keeping them free from want. I enjoy my vocation and the gift of good friends. But all of these are of lesser importance than the greatest gift of all.

When my mother left Sweden to make her way in the new world at age fourteen, her father gave her a Bible. In the front of it he wrote two verses: one from 3 John and one from the Gospel of John. When I went overseas in World War II, my mother gave me a Bible inscribed with the same two verses. They seem to sum up everything that I would hope for in terms of successful priorities for my own children: "I have no greater joy than to know that my children walk in truth" (3 John 4, KJV). "Jesus said . . . , I am the way, the truth, and the life" (John 14:6, KJV). If success, then, is *being* rather than *getting,* walking in the truth—that is, being authentic in following Christ—rather than acquiring wealth and prestige, the marks of success are these: I like who I am when I am following Christ, and I am free to be who I am in my relationships to God, people, and things.

But it is very difficult not to try to hide our true selves because we either don't like ourselves or are afraid others won't.

We Cannot Hide Our Goals for Success

Some time ago I was back visiting in New York City. Walking down one of the interesting side streets that runs off lower Fifth

Avenue, I came to a bookstore with a fantastic display in its shabby window.

Now for me, passing a bookstore window is about as difficult as it must be for an alcoholic to pass a cocktail lounge. But before I began to examine the window display for familiar friends or some potential new friends, I saw a cloth banner hanging on the wall. This is what it said:

You Tell on Yourself

> You tell on yourself by the friends you seek,
> By the very manner in which you speak,
> By the way you employ your leisure time,
> By the use you make of dollar and dime.
>
> You tell what you are by the things you wear,
> By the spirit in which your burdens bear,
> By the kind of things at which you laugh,
> By the records you play on your phonograph.
>
> You tell what you are by the way you walk,
> By the things of which you delight to talk,
> By the manner in which you bear defeat,
> By so simple a thing as how you eat.
>
> By the books you choose from a well-filled shelf;
> In these ways and more, you tell on yourself;
> So there's really no particle of sense
> In an effort to keep up false pretense.
>
> You tell on yourself.

I had to go in and buy that banner. As soon as I returned to my office I hung it on the wall because it reminded me that my true goals for success are revealed to all who really know me.

I love what this piece of verse says, first of all, because it's true. But I love it because it captures in simple, unsophisticated language the whole principle that is just now being emphasized by modern Gestalt psychology that we unconsciously reveal who we are with every gesture and habit.

Of course we tell on ourselves. One does not have to be a depth psychologist to know that how people look, what they wear, how they speak, what they say, and what they don't say tells the whole story. We are walking computers of all of our hopes, disappointments, experiences, fears, prejudices, of all that we have done to others and have allowed them to do to us on our journeys toward success.

Our Bodies "Tell on Us"

One basic underlying truth of Gestalt psychology is that your body cannot lie. Whatever external events you happen to be experiencing are revealed immediately in your physical body.

I have already mentioned the workshop I attended recently led by William Schutz. The main thrust of the workshop had to do with the need for honesty. Talking in the context of Watergate and our national posture, Schutz was able to bring all the implications of that situation down to where each of us lives.

At one point he suggested that we break up into psycho-drama pairs with someone of the opposite sex. Then we were instructed to role-play an imaginary situation in which we were married to each other and in which the husband, unknown to his wife, was having an affair with his secretary. We were to act out a homecoming dialogue between this husband and wife, during which this secret was not to be divulged. For fifteen minutes we acted out what is unfortunately a common scene in many American homes today. After fifteen minutes we switched roles and acted out a similar homecoming scene in which the wife was supposed to be having an affair with her husband's business partner. At the end of these two role-playing situations, Schutz asked for feedback from the audience, specifically in the area of our physical reactions.

Well, it was uncanny. Without exception, everyone who voiced reactions had experienced a growing sense of pain or discomfort. Some people said their feelings centered in the pit of their stomachs which felt leaden or knotted. Others felt their sinuses tightening. Some noticed their throats constricting and their voices becoming strained. Others reported a sense of pressure on their skulls and a great heaviness that was triggering a headache. Well, the point was dramatically illustrated that you cannot live a lie without having it reflected in your body. Now this is not really new. Psychosomatic medicine has been pursuing this truth for a long time. Even the unknown author of my new banner was trying to say the same thing and more. Not just your body, but your whole life-style, the things for which you spend your money—all of these things tell who you are.

Success and Being Who I Am

Ultimately, what all of this says to me is that I need to spend less time trying to cover up who I am. I can stop worrying that someone will betray a confidence I've given or that a group I'm in will prove untrustworthy. For, in point of fact, I walk around as an open book to all who can read.

Surely Jesus' amazing insight about people is the supreme demonstration of all of this. On meeting Nathaniel for the first time he says, "Here is an Israelite worthy of the name; there is nothing false in him" (John 1:47). Before Nathaniel said a single word, Jesus read in him his whole life-style. This was not because he had mystic powers, but simply because he was so free to be himself that he could receive the vibrations of another and respond. Nathaniel, of course, is delighted not just to be described as an Israelite in whom there is nothing false, but as someone who is loved enough by another to be read and to be understood.

The fear that I experience most commonly is the fear of being found out, of being revealed as unloving or dishonest. Well, if any truly discerning person can read who I am, then I can say to God and to myself, "This is who I am." I may not like who I am and I may want to change, but the change that is offered by God in Christ begins when I am free to be who I am.

Jesus Christ is the author and initiator of all changes toward wholeness. To appropriate his love and power to change me, I must first of all stand naked before him and before my fellowman. To realize that my body will not lie means that I am already naked before the discerning, as well as before God. This means being unafraid of being found out. This kind of self-revelation is probably the beginning of the most liberating kind of life that any of us can know. And living that life with others must be close to what it means to begin to be a success as a Christian.

MEMORANDUM

TO: Keith

FROM: Bruce

RE: Chapter Ten—Christian "Success"

Dear Keith:

In my opinion one of the most helpful things you've written has to do with the false criteria for success in the church. You talked about the "ladders" Christians and non-Christians have devised to climb in order to clarify the extent of their success to other people.

I think it would be very helpful to discuss success from that perspective here. And then maybe to give an indication of what you think the shape of success may be for a contemporary Christian man or woman. How do we know when we've succeeded?

Bruce

The Christian's Problem in Dealing with Success

Among the many universal problems a new Christian faces which are hidden in a great cloud of pious silence is the problem of success. What does it mean to be a successful Christian? Since we are told we are to be humble and deny ourselves, it sounds sort of un-Christian even to talk about success for ourselves.

But after our basic physiological needs are met, we human beings do begin to set goals and try to reach them. These goals represent success for us—even if the goal is to be a beachcomber who does nothing. Some of our most basic conflicts come about when we repress our *true* goals because they are not acceptable to our conscious moral or religious standards. For instance, a Christian doctor may want to make a lot of money, but he's been taught to give his services to the Lord and that people in the Lord's service should be poor. So he must get an accountant to handle all his billing, collecting, investing, etc., in order not to "see" himself becoming wealthy. Or a Christian woman secretly wants to be considered sexy and beautiful, though she has been trained that these are not desirable attributes of a pious Christian. So she is very active in church but dresses in a very chic and distracting way. Or a minister or writer who wants to be powerful must rationalize that his manipulation to increase his church's membership or to sell books is a result of the Holy Spirit's guidance toward evangelism.

I do not think it is evil or non-Christian for a doctor to make a good living, for a Christian woman to be attractive, or for ministers or writers to reach large numbers of people. But I think it is dangerous when *any* Christian deceives himself and others as to what his dreams of success really are. For we may find ourselves unwittingly leading other people to our own idols and into the fulfillment of *our* will for their lives, instead of leading them to the healing Christ and the finding of his will.

But what is "success" for the Christian? Let's look for just a moment at the process and criteria the world recognizes as constituting success.

The World's Criteria

In almost all of the academic disciplines and in the professions today, the notions of *growth* and *competence* have a central place in the process which leads toward success. These terms seem to refer to the possession of an increasing amount of knowledge combined with practice or experience until the professional has reached a level considered by his colleagues to be clearly superior. Visible status ladders have been devised for him to climb: grades are given; degrees granted; societies are organized toward which the young professional can aim in order to demonstrate to his profession, the world, and himself that he has personally attained excellence and success in his field. People are called "Doctor," "President," "Senator," "Professor." Others demonstrate their relative competence by the size of their net worth. But since one cannot wear his balance sheet pinned to his lapel, the wealthy have clothes, jewels, houses, cars, boats, airplanes and trips, to indicate where they are on the financial ladder. Professors use degrees, academic titles, research papers, and books.

This status system not only provides ways for the people involved to measure advancement in their fields, but it supplies the motivational power to help the young professional pay the price it takes to get through the long dry years of preparation to reach the higher rungs on the ladder.

Christian Success?

But what does Christian success look like? Here we are in a different world of relatedness. A Christian cannot earn his status, his "righteousness," in his relationship to God with any amount of effort or achievement. The gift of God's love and acceptance is just that—a gift, an unearned gift, to be received or not.

According to the Scriptures, Christ loved us enough to die for us before we even knew about him or wanted to get our relationships straightened out (see Rom. 5:8). If this is true, we certainly did not earn God's love through conscious effort. But because our entire secular lives are regulated by achievement goals and status systems, we in the church have done a strange thing: we have invented invisible status ladders for church members to climb to demonstrate their success as compared to other Christians. The ladders are invisible because we know intuitively that we are not supposed to have them. But they are nevertheless very real—and I believe harmful—since they can keep us from genuine Christian growth and development.

Imagine with your mind's eye your own church's sanctuary with invisible ladders leaning against the walls. You can't see the ladders themselves, just people hanging there at various heights. Everyone who has been around a congregation long knows who the "head honchos," the acknowledged leaders, are. And yet there is often no formal designation of these people as the leading Christians—everyone in the community "just knows" they are on the higher rungs of the congregation's ladder.

Some Christian Ladders

What do these ladders or criteria of growth and achievement look like in your church? If we do not know what the goals and unconsciously accepted directions for growth are, our Christian education efforts will be ineffective. They may be even self-defeating.

I would like to describe a few of these ladders which are accepted, often without examination, as yardsticks for Christian growth and development.[1] In each case it is difficult to criticize the model since there is an important truth involved which relates to Christian maturity. The problem comes when the changed behavior advocated becomes a status symbol of success.

Doing No Wrong. The first ladder is built on the notion that Christian growth or goodness is determined by the "absence of badness" in a person's life. That is, one gets to be a better Christian according to the increasing number of *bad* things he does not do. For instance, if I don't drink, don't smoke, don't commit adultery, and don't dip snuff—and you don't drink, don't smoke, don't commit adultery but you *do* dip snuff, then I'm a better Christian than you are! But if carried to its logical conclusion, what would Christian perfection look like according to this model? Perfection would consist of lying in bed alone—inert—doing nothing! And of course that is a description of death, not life. Christian education programs bent in this direction tend to create a separatist, Pharisaical elite, as people get higher on the ladder.

It is dangerous to talk this way because I believe there are things we should not do, since they can damage our bodies and our relationships to God and people. But to make not doing these things criteria for increasing righteousness is to create a negative doctrine of justification by works, since there is an implication that not doing bad things earns more righteousness.

Doing Good Things. Another ladder model indicates that Christian growth or goodness is determined by the number of good things one does as a Christian. And this is closer to many of us. According to this theory of growth, someone asks the pastor about a member of his congregation, "Is old Joe a good Christian?" The pastor may answer, "Oh, yes, he's in church every Sunday." The next rung on this activities ladder is attendance on Sunday nights, then on Wednesday nights (in churches which still have Wednesday night services). Perhaps the next rung might be teaching a Sunday school class or singing in the choir or leading the men's (or women's) organization of the church or being a deacon or vestryman. But when a lay person has done all these things— clear up to being head of the deacons or senior warden, he may go to his minister and say, "What's the next step, pastor? I want to be Christ's person." And the minister, thinking quickly back over his own ladder, says, "Why, George, you must be called to be a preacher!"

Poor old George is horrified. He may have a speech impediment, hate counseling, or be a very inept leader. Yet, as Kenneth Chafin says, "We take up a collection, package him up, and mail him off to seminary." And often the truth is that the man has no business being an ordained minister. His witness and work as a layman might be much more fulfilling for him—and God. But because of the ladder, he goes to seminary.

Then he discovers that there is a ministerial ladder to tell how he is doing as a pastor, compared to other pastors. It works something like this: You are at a gathering of ordained ministers after you've been out of seminary a few years, and an old classmate walks up. "Where are you serving now, George?" he asks with a concerned look. (It is interesting to note that this question is almost always asked by a man in a large or prestigious church.) Old George stammers, "Arp, Texas."

"Oh, yes, *Arp*. How many people do you have in your congregation there now?"

"Seventy" (including three dogs in the yard and a couple of neighbor kids who play on the property during the service).

"Ummm, well, I'm sure that's a great place to get *experience*." And he proceeds to tell poor old George about his thriving and growing parish. This is called "rung dropping," and it tells the other person that he's lower than you on the ladder of ecclesiastical success.

After being a minister in an important church, the next rung might be to become a district president or superintendent or even a bishop.* Fortunately, the Lord seems to have provided a way to by-pass the ministerial ladder: one can go directly to the mission field from seminary, and even the bishop doesn't know if he is more successful than you.

Please do not misunderstand what I am saying. I think we should attend worship and teach and work in the church, and I thank God for people who are called into the ordained ministry and to the mission field. But to make any of these things a criterion for earning success is to create an idol and a works-righteousness religion. I believe the gospel teaches that a young housewife serving coffee lovingly and happily to a neighbor in Christ's name is just as close to God as a foreign missionary getting shot at in some far corner of the world. It may be noble to go, but most missionaries want to go. And if they are going to earn status with God or men through their poverty or "giving alms in foreign lands," one wonders how effective they could be anyway. I do not believe that the works one does or the status one acquires, as such, confer on him Christian maturity. (Although, paradoxically, it is almost inevitable that a mature Christian will do good works.)

"Knowing" the Faith. A third ladder of growth or success has to do with one's intellectual grasp of the faith. Although I believe that reading and studying can help the process of Christian development immeasurably, intellectual pride is "a natural" for ladder-climbers.

According to this theory, a person who knows more about his faith is thought to be more mature and closer to God. This ladder has a conservative and a liberal side. The conservative might feel

---

* Each denomination has the rungs named differently, but every one I've checked *has* the ladder—even the Quakers with their "weighty friends" and those not so weighty.

Christian "Success" / 201

that the more Bible verses he has memorized, the more mature he is. I have known some people who seemed to feel compelled to quote Scriptures when they met. Instead of saying "Good morning," they were more likely to say, "John 3:16." But in the building where my oil business friends have offices if you greeted them with "John 3:16," some men would think you were talking about the rest room on the third floor. These conspicuous Scripture quoters have a quotation for every remark.

Again, I hope you will not misunderstand what I am saying. I take the Scriptures very seriously, and I have many verses memorized. I find this helpful as an aid in living and as an index telling me where major themes of the faith are portrayed and discussed. And I use the Scriptures continually in teaching. But to make my ability and willingness to memorize and quote the criteria for growth and wholeness is, I believe, to misunderstand the gospel.

It has always been interesting to me to note that although Jesus used allusions to the Scriptures, he is reported to have quoted them primarily in his encounters with Satan (e.g., Matt. 4:1–11), when teaching and giving them a new interpretation (e.g., Matt. 5–7; 19:3–9, 26:31), or in direct confrontations when rebuking those who were unreal (e.g., Matt. 15:7–9). When talking to the people, he told stories about life to illustrate what God's purposes and reign would be like. Matthew (13:34) claimed that Jesus only used parables when speaking to the people (see Matt. 13:3–9, 18–23, 24–30, 31–32, 33, 44, 45–46, 47–50; 18:23–35; 20:1–16; 21:33–45; 22:1–14; 25:1–13, 14–30, 31–46.)*

These things indicate to me that though the Scriptures were used for teaching purposes, they were not meant to be displayed as marks of righteousness. As a matter of fact, the Pharisees were criticized by Jesus for the pride they showed in carrying "Bible verses" prominently displayed in their phylacteries (Matt. 23:5).†

---

* Since Matthew's bias was certainly in the direction of reference to Scripture, I checked only the first Gospel to give a general picture of the ways Jesus is reported to have communicated.

† I have a few friends who quote the Bible continually and use this as an effective method of witnessing and evangelism. They are exceptional people and are so immersed in the Scriptures it seems natural for them. But for every one of these there are ten who come across to me as exhibitionists or users of an "in" language. I suppose I am making such a strong point about this because the Bible has meant so much to me, and I was almost driven away from it as a new Christian by a legalistic Bible quoter.

On the liberal side of the knowledge ladder Christians play "have you read?" Those who can discuss the latest book casting some light on the theological or psychological aspects of the faith are considered by this group to be the most mature Christians. At a meeting one man will insert into a conversation, "Last night I was reading Myron Madden's new book, *Raise the Dead!* By the way, have you read it yet?" And the other Christian, defensive, not wanting to be considered out of it, mumbles something like, "Well, I've heard of it. As a matter of fact, I think I have it, but I haven't had a chance to read it yet." And the other person says, "Oh, well, there's no reason you should have read it. No one can read *everything*" (especially down there on the rung you're on. Of course, I'm busy too, but I managed to read it). And so it goes.

This ladder of knowledge about the faith seems to be the principal criterion for Christian growth and success used in almost all theological seminaries, conservative and liberal.

Other Ladders. There are many other status ladders which we Christians are climbing and using as criteria with which to determine our own growth and to judge and dismiss those who are lower or not even on our ladder. For example, increasing poverty, social action involvement, and competitive honesty.

But if none of these ladders necessarily lead to maturity, then what does constitute success for the committed Christian?

A Holy Spirit Ladder? After trying to climb several of the Christian ladders, I got discouraged. And then some people told me I needed the filling of the Holy Spirit. This would come when I committed my life as totally as I could to Jesus Christ as *Lord* (instead of only Savior) and asked him to fill my life with his Spirit. He would then give me the gifts I needed to do his will. If I did that, I was told, I would lead a "victorious life" and be able to handle all my problems. I made this second commitment and opened my life. Things went well for a while, but I realized finally I was on a "Holy Spirit ladder." For instance, if I had the gift of teaching and someone else did not, I was "more spiritual." If they had one I didn't, I wanted it and felt a little second class if I didn't have it. This led to anxious feelings.

I also discovered that if I have a life with "all victories," it means that I am almost certainly repressing many of my honest feelings and responses. I saw that all I can do is offer my real feelings to God, then if they are un-Christian, to tell him it is my desire not to act out these feelings. But then I must go about the business of trying to change my *behavior,* waiting on God's timing as to *when* and *if* my feelings will change.

As a student of psychology and as a Christian, I knew that one cannot force his feelings to change—even for God's sake. The psychologist Jolande Jacobi, speaking for Carl Jung, said that "the widely prevailing view that psychic development leads ultimately to a state in which there is no suffering is of course utterly false. Suffering and conflict are a part of life; they must not be regarded as 'ailments'; they are the natural attributes of all human existence, the normal counterpole, so to speak, of happiness. Only when from weakness, cowardice, or lack of understanding the individual tries to evade them do ailments and complexes arise." [2]

After trying both consciously and unconsciously to earn or manipulate God's increasing approval in my direction in all the ways I've described, I began to realize that I had deeply misunderstood the question of being successful as a Christian.

Christian Success—A Moving Process?

In the Gospels we see Jesus speaking of success—indeed of the victories of faith—but also of persecution, renunciation, and poverty. His own life was the story of his becoming the particular man in and through whom God could live out the unique task only Jesus could fulfill. He spoke of and demonstrated failure and recovery. He knew a kind of ultimate defeat and rejection at the cross. And the majority of the world of his time who saw his defeat *never accepted* the subsequent victory of the resurrection. So in the eyes of most of his contemporaries he was a fake or at least a total failure who lost his cause in a resounding defeat. But his life and purposes went on invisibly through his spirit embodied in his followers—in the church.

What does all this say about success as a Christian? To me it says that success is not reaching a specific goal or status but a kind of becoming of that which we were designed to *be* for the particular work God has for us to *do.* As William Temple said, we become discouraged because "we do not see the outline of the finished product in our lives. But this is not the way God works. In looking at an acorn no one can see the outline of an oak tree—yet it is contained in the acorn."³ I believe that what we call success is part of a process, a journey with the living God toward becoming his persons and doing his will.

As Paul Tournier has said it, "God has a purpose: the entire Bible proclaims this. What matters is that his plan [involving us] should be understood and fulfilled. So, in the light of the Bible, the problem is shifted onto new ground. The question is no longer whether one is succeeding or failing but whether one is fulfilling God's purpose or not, whether one is adventuring with him or against him. It is, of course, always a joyful thing to succeed. But the joy is very deceptive if it comes from the satisfaction of an ambition that is contrary to the will of God. And of course failure is still very painful; but the pain is fruitful if it is part of God's purpose. A failure, within God's purpose, is no longer really a failure." ⁴

Chapter Eleven

Change, Risk and Growth

MEMORANDUM

TO: Keith
FROM: Bruce
RE: Chapter Eleven—Change, Risk and Growth

Dear Keith:

    Your part of the Chapter on "Christian Success" just arrived. You have indicated that growth is not a status but a process. Why don't you continue by answering the question: "What does the **actual process** of changing and growing look like—if it's not climbing ladders?" How do you see growth as a process? Can you give any scriptural support for this view? What makes one dare to risk change in a way which helps growth take place? And maybe you could get into the kind of self-examination a serious Christian might undertake if he were interested in trying to grow toward being more nearly Christ's person and companion on the adventure.

                                                                 Bruce

WHEN I realized that "success" in the Christian life is not climbing ladders, I began to wonder how the *process* of growth might take place. About that time I was reading a book by Paul Tournier called *A Place for You*.¹ As I was reading I began to realize why Christian "progress" on the adventure with God is not reaching a pinnacle, or ladder-climbing, or straining neurotically for doctrinal or moral purity, or ecstatic experiences.

Surrendering Our False Gods

I began to grasp the notion that Christian growth may take place through continuing to surrender our more ultimate securities to God as they are revealed to us. We begin at conversion by renouncing the flimsy but familiar security of our pagan existence: the taking the role of God in our own vocational or social worlds. As we turn our backs on the past, we realize that we have tried to build a life on the shifting sand of our achievements.

But almost immediately, it seems, we begin to build, instead, a new controllable security by climbing one of the Christian status ladders. And when we see that we have started building a competitive kingdom again, we must surrender and repent.

If this is true, then Christian growth may take place through an "endless" series of turning loose of our more controllable securities as ultimate. In the act of turning loose we reach out with a leap of faith, which is always frightening, always to some degree anxiety-provoking. And with newly freed hands we can reach out creatively to touch God's people in healing ways.

Pierre Teilhard de Chardin has indicated that this kind of relinquishment is a perfect preparation for death. For at the end of life the Christian who has surrendered all material and status securities as ultimate has only to turn loose of the body to be unencumbered in joining God.

A Scriptural View

But is this scriptural—this idea that growth takes place through taking the risk of changing our directions or plans by surrendering abilities, status, techniques, and awards? Are we supposed to release these things which are less than God but which we have clutched to save ourselves and build ourselves up? Tournier suggests that this view is biblical.[2] Look at Abraham. He was a man who evidently had a secure place with his father in Ur and then in Haran. But the Scriptures indicate that God asked him to turn loose of that place and go to a foreign land in which his safety and future would be uncertain. He did, and God gave him the security of a new place in what was to become Palestine.

Then Abraham wanted the assurance of the continuation of his "name" through a son. And in his old age he and Sarah had a son. In at least one way, this son meant more to Abraham than a son might to a Christian today. At that time, the idea of heaven was not a part of the Hebrews' thinking. Heaven was, as I understand it, a rather late idea in biblical history. When an ancient Hebrew died, the only afterlife he had to look forward to might be the vague land of shadows (*Sheol*). His only hope to live beyond his own death was through a son. So in the story when Abraham was asked to sacrifice his son, Isaac, on the altar, it was something like asking him to give up his only child, and heaven too. And his willingness to risk turning loose of this kind of security in order to trust God made him the model of the man of faith for all future generations (see Rom. 4:1–25).

A similar pattern unfolds in the life of Moses. He was raised in a position of affluence and power, but was confronted by God with risking his position to help his own people. After much struggling with God and himself, he turned loose and went. And finally, at the end of his adventures in the wilderness, just as he was arriving at the promised destination, he was asked to surrender his place with the people and not to go into Palestine with them. Moses did let go, and he became the greatest spiritual hero of the Jewish people. He and Abraham seemed to grow in spiritual stature each time they risked their security and took a new leap of faith in trying to do what they felt was God's will with their lives.

In Jesus' life there is a similar struggle and outcome. At Gethsemane Jesus evidently felt that his ministry was at stake. A week earlier the people had welcomed him into Jerusalem with palm branches, hailing him as the Messiah. He was apparently fulfilling his dream, and was being accepted by the people. And yet at Gethsemane Jesus evidently heard God saying, "Change your whole game plan, risk turning loose of your ministry and mission, and trust their safety and yours to me alone." Three times the Scriptures indicate that Jesus tried to talk God out of that course. But the call was to "turn loose." He did. And the Christian church is here bearing his name at least partially because he did surrender that night.

Turning Loose of the Trapeze

A Christian, according to this view of Tournier's, is like a person hanging from a trapeze bar. And that bar is whatever your security is truly invested in—though a Christian often consciously believes that his security is in Christ. But in my case, my true trust has most often been in things like social acceptance, my ability to communicate and my ability to earn a decent living. Most of my deepest concentration and time have been occupied in enhancing and protecting those things which constitute my real, though often unconscious, securities at any given time. And growth takes place when God swings another trapeze bar in view. The new trapeze might be a vocational challenge, a chance to be more honest in my work or to risk financial security in order to do his will. The "bar" coming toward me might be a sense of calling to lead a more disciplined life with Christ, or help some oppressed people—and risk rejection.

But there are at least two basic problems we face as we are confronted by a call to relinquish our present equilibrium and reach out. One difficulty is that the new challenge (which will be the scene of our security later) usually appears at first as a frightening threat. To grasp any new situation which will change our security base, it seems that one must let go of the old. The new trapeze bar swings toward me just far enough from the present one that I cannot hang on to the old with one hand and grab the new with the other. So each new opportunity to grow carries with it a decision to surrender an old security as ultimate in order to place one's trust more deeply in God's hands. And the risk is always frightening, if a real security is at stake. There is inevitably a kind of death involved in each significant spurt of growth.*

---

* Just a word of caution for Christian leaders who may take this position seriously. Some people are far more prone to risk than others. Each person has a particular pace and rhythm at which he grows and learns best. And

People have paid thousands of dollars over the centuries to watch trapeze artists, not because it is difficult to hang from a bar. They pay for that one second when the performer lets go and reaches out for the next bar. Will he fall? And I believe that's our question in the church! I think many of us want to surrender our flimsy securities and reach ahead for a deeper and more personal involvement with God and his people—with life. But we are afraid that if we turn loose, we will fall into an unknown condition and lose what we have—and we cannot chance it.

What Makes Us Willing to Risk?

But if this willingness to change and risk—this turning loose and reaching out—is the course of Christian growth for people seeking to discover themselves and God's will, what provides the motivation to move ahead?

In World War II it was demonstrated through experimental testing that men going into combat learned directions and remembered instructions with amazing speed and retention. It seems that we learn and remember things when *our own personal destinies* are wrapped up in our learning and remembering them. And my experience has been that I am generally willing to be vulnerable to change my habits and plans and risk myself for other people only when my destiny and relationship with God seem to depend on this kind of vulnerability.

Some Side Effects of Risking Change

This turning loose and risking has some amazing educational

---

there is also a kind of neurotic risking in order to prove one's self. Such people need to hear a very different message: "Growth for you may be to realize that you do *not* have to earn your acceptance by your incessant risking." For a Christian leader to try to force risking on the part of others is neither effective nor safe in my opinion. The leader can risk in his own life and can tell stories of others' risking. But he should realize that not only is each individual evidently different from others with regard to the size, frequency, or even possibility of his risking, but that there is also a rhythm of growth and withdrawal within any given life. Pierre Teilhard de Chardin in *The Divine Milieu* (New York: Harper & Row, 1968, p. 94) said, "There is a time for growth and a time for diminishment in the lives of each one of us. At one moment the dominant note is one of constructive human effort, and at another mystical annihilation" (see also Eccles. 3:1–9).

side effects. When I step forward and become vulnerable to people out of gratitude to God for saving my sanity and loving me, then I am forced back to a deeper interior prayer life and to reading the Scriptures and consulting honestly with my Christian friends. Because when I really risk, I am over my head, out of my depth, and I need more power and insight in order to survive each day. When I study or hear sermons at such times, I am highly motivated and much more likely to retain what I am reading or hearing.

As Kenneth Chafin has said, "We pray for power in the church all the time, but we don't need more power to do most of the safe things we do in the church—just more money and volunteers." But when we must have power and discernment, we pray for it and work for it. And that's when it seems to come.

If a Christian is consciously in need of God, because he is risking his safety even in small personal ways, he is highly motivated to learn what the tools and content of his faith are. And the knowledge he gains from this process will be the foundation for new insights leading to further growth and change.

The Process of Turning Loose

But what does turning loose feel like for the one growing?

If it is true that Christian growth involves risking, then what inner process does one go through to discover and release a security which has become more important than doing God's will?*

Sometimes a challenge has been presented to me in a specific and unavoidable way from an external source. For instance, an invitation to teach communication and counseling at a particular graduate school arrived. I had to decide whether the proposed opportunity was right enough for me to rip up my family by the roots for the seventeenth time. An emotional involvement and decision to risk had been precipitated from "the outside" by way of the invitation to teach.

But what if one is restless with his life and ministry, would like to analyze his present priorities and security base, but no confrontation comes from the outside? How would he go about it?

---

* The participants in the human potential movement in psychology have shown us that significant behavioral change by an individual involves not only intellectual understanding but often also emotional commitment, vulnerability, and the process of personal risking (e.g., see Carl Rogers *On Encounter Groups* [New York: Harper & Row, 1970]).

Strangely, I have found something akin to the crisis leading to conversion in each new episode involving the possibility of growth. As this statement implies, I believe significant Christian growth is sporadic and comes as a result of major or minor confrontations and decisions.*

I am finding that over the years I must die to many succeeding idols and securities as I discover that they have become the fortresses behind which I protect myself as god in life (see Luke 9:23, 24). The maintenance of these securities makes me overly cautious. And protecting myself keeps me from the vulnerability of walking unarmed into people's hearts and lives. But I resist the process of risking. And at each point of growth or release I want to stop and build a permanent "home" to live in. I keep forgetting to "consider how the lilies grow in the field" (Matt. 6:28).

Digging Up Hidden Idols

A first step to try to discover what my own protected security might be has been *self-examination*. I have asked myself: "What, next to God, is the most important asset or relationship which I'd hate most to face the future without?"† I've even found it helpful to list the most important things in my life on a piece of paper.‡

But what if a Christian discovers that he *has* made a security idol out of something good which is less than God? He begins to realize, then, that his attachment to that person or thing he worships will become the "price" of his integrity. A minister who worships his parish ministry will get involved in social issues such as race

---

* Even a decision to take a class in school involves a commitment of time and the risk of failure. One must release his security as a nonfailer in that subject to enter the class. The growth takes place through the work following as well as in the decision. But the decision process and initial leap set it off. According to Seward Hiltner, the first thing we know about religious development is that, whatever its specific nature, it is not a mere unfolding— "it has spurts, plateaus, dips. It contains optimal occasions" (*Pastoral Counseling* [New York: Abingdon, 1949]).

† Because of my own history of repression and denial with regard to admitting that I am playing God, I've found it helpful to give God first place in asking the question, realizing that whatever *I* list as *second* is very likely even more important than God to me *as a priority motivating my actual behavior.*

‡ Refer to chapter five, pp. 105–8, for ways to tell what your unconscious priorities may be.

Change, Risk and Growth / 213

relations, for instance, only until his involvement threatens the security of those parishioners who might negatively affect his ministry. A worshiping mother will let her son have all the freedom he wants to grow until his choices threaten her vision of what the child should be.

What can be done when a person sees that the basic focus of his interest and security is centered on something less than God? The second step for me seems to be *confession*. I have to admit to myself and to God that I want my own will for me and the people around me. And I must face the fact that I am clinging to and protecting an idol—my ability, my work, a relationship, a goal—as my real security in which I'm putting my faith and energy. In other words, I have to tell God that I really love and trust something more than him *just as I did when I first came to him*—and this is very humiliating for a person who's been a Christian for years.

One of my own most recent idols has been writing. I have found that I have a fantasy of wanting to be a famous writer. At first I laughed at this as a normal kind of thought for an egomaniac who has had a book published. But as the thought recurred, I quit laughing. I found that I was getting angry with anyone who interrupted my writing, whereas I had always been open to people coming to me for help or to visit. I got impatient with my family. And I began resenting those parts of my work not connected directly with writing. But I continued doing all the traveling, speaking, and other things I'd been doing.

Finally I got miserable enough to stop and see what had happened—I had very subtly and unconsciously made "becoming an outstanding writer" the highest value in my life. Since this was my god, all other values and relationships had to be brought in line with it. My family, friends, students, and strangers had either to support my god or be somehow pushed into the background. And they were. But it all turned sour in my mouth and made me frustrated and very lonely in a way I didn't understand.

Eventually I came to the point at which I realized that writing had become my bet for ultimate security—instead of God and his grace. My knuckles were white from clinging to that "trapeze bar" —the dream of being a great writer. I had a terrible time admitting this to myself. I said, "This is ridiculous. Of course I love God more. I'm just a dedicated writer, that's all." But my behavior gave me away. So I finally confessed: "God, I would like to be an outstanding writer more than I want to be your person." This sounds so childish and naïve as I write it. And I almost did not tell you. But I think the subtlety and unacceptable nature of our idolatry is part of the reason we haven't been able to face it in the church.

The third step I think one takes is to *surrender again*—totally: "God, I want you more than I want to be an outstanding writer. I want to know you and do your will, trusting you with the outcome of my efforts and my life." But the first time I started to say those words about writing, I realized I could not say them honestly. As stupid as it sounds, there was a stubborn knot in my insides which said, "No, I'm not giving this up to you, God. I want it for me—even if it ruins my life."

But I knew myself well enough to know it would ruin my life if I kept it in the number one position. So I finally said, "God, I can't turn loose of my dream. But I want to. I give it up to you by intention and give you permission to come into the deeper layers of my personality and help me turn loose and reach toward you for my ultimate security and meaning. I want to write if it's your will, but I want to become your person more." I realized in that moment that I had committed everything over which I had control to God.

I am finding that my "place" in which I can hope to risk and change is not a committed status at which I arrived through conversion. Nor is it the top of a ladder of works I've performed. My "place," paradoxically, is not a "destination" at all. But it feels like a moving journey, a changing pilgrimage with a group of broken but joyous becomers. We are weak and yet know the power that comes from being personal. We have been broken, in that our kingdoms have been surrendered. And yet we are in the process of changing and becoming whole as we reach out with open and creative hands toward people, work, and God.

MEMORANDUM

TO: Bruce
FROM: Keith
RE: Chapter Eleven—Change, Risk and Growth

Dear Bruce:

I realize after reading through the material I just sent that people might get the idea we **only** grow spiritually by giving up idols. But of course that is **not** true. There are many other ways to grow, as well as other reasons to risk changing behavior.

Why don't you include something about other causes for taking the risk of changing? And talk about change itself and how it is related to risking. Once you told me about the way your own attitude was turned around when you discovered that you could "choose" rather than just react. That was very helpful to me in seeing how much more fun a "choosing" life can be, even if one's **circumstances** haven't been altered a bit.

Keith

The Need for Change

In February of 1973 a man was working on his farm in Wisconsin when suddenly something dropped out of the sky onto the field near him. It was blue, pockmarked, frozen, and mysterious. Excitedly, he chopped off a huge chunk, put it in his deep freeze, and called the sheriff and some geologists from the nearby college to examine it.

For a long time they were all stumped. Was it a meteor? Was it a piece of glacier carried by the jet stream? The only thing they were sure of at the time was that it was frozen hard, and when it melted, it smelled terrible! Much later, someone solved the mystery. It turned out to be blue "potty fluid" accidentally ejected from an airplane toilet.

You know, if I were that man who had received that mysterious gift from heaven, I would probably have done just what he did. I would gather up as much of it as I could to preserve in my deep freeze. And I suspect that over the years a great many things have dropped into my life from out of the blue that I have treated just like that. I have assumed that everything that seems to come from heaven is a gift of God.

So many of our customs and traditions are like that. Sometimes even the life-style or vocation in which we find ourselves fits that category. A family business left by a generous father or a vocation chosen by a well-meaning mother can turn out to be smelly, frozen, and pockmarked, and not God's gift at all.

The tragic person is the one who will preserve his freezer full of "blue ice" at all costs and defend it against all charges. Probably many people have a freezer full of such ice cubes. But one should be able, from time to time, to examine what he is preserving and eliminate that which seems unnecessary or harmful. However, this calls for change—a painful process for most of us.

Why Do We Resist Change?

Why do we resist change? Why is it painful? It seems to me that most of us find change difficult, if not almost impossible, because of our preoccupation with preserving or defending the past. The Copernican revolution is a classic example of this tendency among Christians.

You will recall that Copernicus came up with the idea that there was a basic flaw in the current understanding of the whole astronomical system. He said, in effect, "Gentlemen, let me suggest that the sun doesn't revolve around the earth; the earth revolves around the sun."

It took him seventeen years to perfect the theory, and another thirteen years to find a printer who would publish it. It wasn't until after his death that this basic truth was accepted.

If you consider yourself a reactionary, you're in good company. The great churchmen of those days ridiculed Copernicus. Martin Luther said, "This fool will turn the art of astronomy upside down. . . . The Scripture shows and tells another lesson, where Joshua commanded the sun to stand still, not the earth." John Calvin asked, "Who will venture to place the authority of Copernicus above that of the Holy Spirit?" The Vatican damned the Copernican theory as both "philosophically false and formally heretical."

For some reason there is a tendency among Christians to want to look back—to glamorize the past or hold to some outmoded truth, even using the Bible as the authority for preventing change. We are caught in the tension between preserving the good from the past and embracing the new.

Almost seventy years ago, William James, one of America's great pioneer psychologists, said, "Any new theory first is attacked as absurd; then it is admitted to be true, but obvious and insignificant; finally—it seems to be important, so important that its adversaries claim that they themselves discovered it."

What he says so beautifully here is that each of us has in him a bit of the reactionary—some of us to a marked degree.

Changing Is Not Optional—and Is Sometimes Harmful

Whether we are basically innovators or reactionaries, there is no possibility for health or life without change. But not all change is good. Some change is unhealthy and a mark of decay and deterioration.

Profound medical and psychological effects of change have been uncovered. Dr. Thomas H. Holmes of the University of Washington School of Medicine worked with Dr. Richard Rahe to measure these effects. Holmes rated each life-change event such as the death of a loved one, a change of jobs, moving to a new home, etc., according to the amount of impact such an event would have upon a person's life. His study proved that when too many changes come to any person at any given time, the resulting trauma produces physical illness and even death.

The human body and mind and spirit simply cannot handle too much change at one time. And in the past thirty years we have all had to handle so much change that it is no wonder we talk nostalgically about the good old days. Everything around us is changing so radically.

But with all our resistance to change and all the perils of change, it is nevertheless unavoidable. To live is to change. The opposite of change is rigidity, inflexibility. To be alive is to be dynamic and adaptable. This is true for any person, organism, or movement. Arnold Toynbee says, "Civilization is a movement and not a condition, a voyage not a harbor." Medically, doctors look for movement and activity as a sign that the patient is getting well.

Recently in the Georgetown section of Washington, all traffic was stopped near a local boutique where two live people were standing in the window acting as mannequins. The effect was so bizarre and stark that it caused a sensation. People were struck by the spectacle of living people being paid to act like nonhumans. Conceived as a gimmick to sell clothes, it seemed instead to be a tragic parable of what life can become at its worst—flexible people frozen into rigidity.

Listen to what C. S. Lewis says about real spiritual life. "A statue has the shape of a man but it is not alive. In the same way, man has the 'shape' or likeness of God but he has not got the kind of life God has."

He suggested that this is precisely what Christianity is about. This world is a great sculptor's shop. We are the statues, and there is a rumor going around the shop that some of us are going to "come to life." [3]

I think that says it quite well. To live with the kind of hope of coming alive in a new dimension in God's likeness means that we look forward to a form of spiritual change which will be ours as God's people.

Change Involves Risk

Tom Wolfe, one of our most popular writers, said in 1972, "The old dream of the alchemist was to turn base metals into gold. Today he dreams of changing his personality."

To change one's basic personality! This is impossible according to most personality theorists, even with the help of the most excellent psychologist or school. But God gives us the promise and the hope that we can change our behaviors and relationships in some striking ways here and now. However, it will involve some risk-taking. We can no longer play it safe.

Before World War II, when I was a boy we had a stock reply to any and all invitations: "I don't care." If someone said to you, "Do you want to go to the movies?" or "Do you want an ice cream cone?" or "Do you want seconds on dessert?" we youngsters of the thirties and forties would often answer, "I don't care."

What we really meant was, "Of course I do. What a silly question! Anybody would want that. But I am afraid that you will change your mind, or that there are some strings on it, or that there will not be enough when I get there, so I am going to play it safe and say, 'I don't care.' "

Although kids today don't seem to resort to this same subterfuge, all of us still have countless ways of trying to appear invulnerable, to keep from being hurt. Risk-taking is difficult, even for Christians.

Do I "Have To" or "Want To"?

I got a new insight into the dynamics of risk-taking through a friend of mine, a young business executive. He had attended a management conference where an exciting concept was presented. My friend, a new Christian, could immediately see the application for his life.

He learned that good management comes from leaders who have moved beyond the level of saying "I have to" to "I want to." Management consultants feel that people who are always motivated by the "have to" syndrome are poor leaders.

The fact is, nobody ever really has to do anything. You don't have to go to work; you can lose your job. You don't have to pay taxes; you can go to jail. You don't have to stay married; you can leave your spouse and pay the consequences. You don't have to be a parent; the state can put your children in foster homes. The list goes on and on.

The conversation with my friend helped me realize how often I have fallen into the trap of "have to." How many times I have told my family, "I have to be in Cincinnati this weekend" or "I have to go to Baltimore and speak at a meeting" or "I have to see someone at the office for counseling tonight."

What does this communicate? It gives a picture to my family of some mean tyrant forcing me to do things I don't want to do. If they love me, they will resent my colleagues or God himself. For surely someone is responsible for all of these things that friend, husband, or father "has to" do.

But even more, how does this attitude affect me as I keep these engagements that I feel I "have to" keep?

The things my friend learned may apply in some ways to all of us. Ideally we should not have anything on our calendar that we feel we have to do. The things that take our time should be the things we really want to do. If it is not something we can honestly say we want to do, then we should think about consciously "choosing" to do it over the alternatives. In my job responsibilities, for instance, having weighed both sides of the situation and wanting to keep my job, I can choose to see a particular person or go on a particular trip. I don't have to, but I choose to.

Risking and Choosing with Other Christians

Let me say a word now to some of you housewives who feel trapped in a role that traditionally has been left to women. If you don't want to make beds or clean toilets or scrub floors, what are your choices? Well (if you don't want to run away), you can live in a dirty house, or get a job and hire someone to make your beds and clean your floors and toilets. Or you can lay it on your family to pitch in and help. While some of you may never be in the "want to" role about housework, at least you can be in the "choose to." This means that you prefer housework to the alternatives.

How does all this fit into risk-taking? It seems to me that there are obvious examples of risk-taking in life, such as getting married or buying stocks or starting a new job. None of these are certainties. Every time we drive down the highway, we take the risk that there may be a drunken or irresponsible driver threatening our lives. Living is not a sure thing.

Change, Risk and Growth / 221

At a deeper level, becoming a Christian is taking a risk. There is no way to know what Christ will do with our lives. Coming under his management means that we take the risk of having a New Boss who may require job changes, personality changes, attitude changes, and financial risks. As Christians, we are asked to team up with people wherever we live who can together seek the will of God and be available to him. This teaming with people is in some ways even more risky than trusting Christ. The things he asks of me I know I will find bearable and possible, and even enjoyable most of the time, because he is trustworthy. But when he asks me to trust a group of people like me with my secrets, my plans, my hopes, my dreams, and my life, it is much more dangerous. And that's exactly the point. Trying to be the Body of Christ with people who are no more dependable than ourselves means risk-taking!

But for the Christian, real risk-taking involves even more. It involves trusting the voice of God inside us. It means doing only things that we really want to do or choose to do. And as we do this God is making us more sensitive and freeing us to choose more nearly according to what we can determine to be his will. It means eliminating the things we have to do for wrong reasons.

When we have become Christians and have received a new spirit, God puts into us a desire to do his will. This does not mean necessarily that we become perfect people, or even that we perform better. The "new creation" is made up of persons who now *want* to do the thing that God wants them to do. We move away from the "oughts" and "have tos" into the "want tos" and "choose tos" of life, and thus become free and spiritually contagious people.

There is safety in living by oughts and have tos. If we do things because of family pressure or because of a boss or because of some stern God, then we have a built-in excuse for failure. We can tell ourselves we failed because we never wanted to do that. It was something we had to do. If you fail, however, in doing the thing that deep down inside you want to do, then you have no one to blame. This may be the kind of radical risk-taking to which Christ calls us.

Risking and Security

We need to leave the security of the "have to" style of life. The Bible tells us about a man who was asked to become a disciple. When he tells Jesus that he wants to follow him but asks first to go and bury his father, Jesus replies in harsh words, "Leave the dead to bury their dead" (Luke 9:57–60) You and I may know people who say that they would certainly have been missionaries except for all the things they had to do—they had an aged parent who needed them, or they had to raise a family, or they had to put children through college. So they could not embark on a risky venture. On the other hand, one man I know gave up his secure job in business for a risky job in mission. His family unanimously urged him to take the risk. It has brought them all into new levels of love and commitment.

Life is full of risk. The Christian life is especially so. For Christians it is all right to fail, but it is not all right not to risk. Launching out into a new venture that you really want to do and that you feel God wants you to do is creative risk-taking at its very best.

On a recent trip to Burmuda my wife and I took off on two bikes for a day's excursion. We arrived at the old harbor in St. George's just in time to see a most unusual sight. Five or six grizzled commercial fishermen were gathered around the wharf watching a young man shove off in an old, clinker-built, double-ender sailboat slightly over twenty feet long. The sails were patched and the rigging looked worn. "You know where that crazy buzzard is going?" one man volunteered. "He's sailing to England in that thing." And as the little boat pulled out from the harbor, those veteran sailors shook their heads in scorn and disbelief.

But somehow the sight of that one frail craft with its lone crew stirred something deep inside of me, and without meaning to, I found myself waving and shouting, "Bon Voyage!" Surprised and encouraged, the young captain waved back and continued to do so until the little boat was gone from sight.

For that young man, getting there wasn't the important thing. He didn't have to make it, but somehow he had to start out. He would not be the man that he was meant to be in the present if he didn't set his sights in the future for that ridiculous and seemingly impossible trip.

I think that's what life is all about. Whether we arrive or not at some future goal isn't the issue. It's O.K. to fail as long as you launch out. We dare not stay in the harbor.

Chapter Twelve

Sickness and Death

MEMORANDUM

TO: Bruce
FROM: Keith
RE: Chapter Twelve—Sickness and Death

Dear Bruce:

Sickness and death are very baffling things to me. But the way we Christians repress our feelings about them is very surprising. We seem to avoid the starkness of human mortality in all sorts of ingenious ways. How about answering questions like: Do you believe God can heal the sick? If so, why are some people so irritating who insist that "every sick person could get well if they were properly prayed for"? What do you think the role of a Christian healer is? What do you believe is the relation between the mind and the body? And can these be reconciled? Finally, what can we do or say about death that is constructive to the living?

Keith

Can God Heal the Sick?

Not long ago I attended a luncheon meeting at a large state hospital. The doctors and medical students present were mostly church members. We had come together to talk about healing. The question of spiritual healing came up, and someone asked if I believe in it. I said I did because God had caught my attention in this area many years ago. It happened during my days as a seminary student when I was serving a small parish on the Hudson River.

One of the parishioners, a woman named Elsie, had a tremendous faith in Christ and a firsthand experience of his power to heal. Elsie had been hospitalized following an injury. And one Saturday night as I made my usual weekend rounds, she greeted me by climbing out of bed and getting onto her crutches.

"Follow me," she said, and as we walked down the hospital corridor together, she told me about a young man who had been in a coma for six days. He'd been racing his car down a local road at more than one hundred miles per hour when the car hit some obstacle and crashed. He had not recovered consciousness.

Elsie had been visiting with the young man's mother. She was from another city and the family priest had not been able to visit the hospital. Elsie assured the mother that when I came I would see her son and pray for his healing.

This terrified me. Up to that point I had not believed that the Lord who healed in the New Testament days was available for healing today. But what could I do? Elsie introduced me to the mother—who, by the way, spoke almost no English—and said cheerily, "Here is my preacher; he will pray for your son."

A nurse was on duty beside the young man's bed, an excellent nurse but one who had previously exhibited a great mistrust and dislike for Christians in general and for clergymen in particular!

There we were, a hostile nurse, a mother who could not communicate, a boy in a coma who could not hear, and a scared young seminary student. The conditions for healing seemed all wrong.

The only thing God had going for him was one woman who believed. As we approached the bed, Elsie said, "Here he is, pray for him."

I remember that I first prayed silently, asking God to help me know what to do. Next, I laid my hands on the boy's foot and said something like, "Lord Jesus, we know that you are here and we ask you to heal this young man."

Before the prayer was over, the boy opened his eyes and said to me, "Hi, Charlie." I mumbled that I wasn't Charlie, but that I was a friend and was glad to see him.

Of the people in that room only Elsie was not surprised. She said, "Well, that's over. Let's go now." I followed her out the door, almost unable to walk.

Chuckling over this story, several of the doctors began to recount similar stories of how God got their attention in the area of spiritual healing while they were still unbelievers.

Then one doctor said, "I believe in spiritual healing, but what irks me is people who go around wanting to pray for everyone to get well." He went on to explain, "I am thinking of a woman who came back from a Christian conference some months ago where she had been healed of arthritis through prayer. Now she wants to run all over the church and my hospital praying for people to get well, and I resent it."

Can Healers Be Overzealous?

In the lively discussion that followed, the question was raised, "Why do we resent this kind of person who tries to force spiritual healing on everyone?" We finally concluded that this approach violates personhood. Jesus did not seek out people to heal. They came to him and asked for healing for themselves, for a friend, or for a member of the family. None were refused. The only time Jesus initiated healing was at the pool of Bethesda. Even then he asked, "Do you want to be healed?" (see John 5).

Our conversation about spiritual healing ended with this self-appraising question: "What is distinctive about a Christian doctor, as contrasted to a good doctor who is not a Christian?" Our consensus was that a Christian has no special medical skills that are unavailable to other colleagues, except for prayer.

But beyond that, we began to see that in many situations we

clergymen and physicians are like the woman who went about determined to heal people by her prayers, violating the personhood of many, though used of God to bring healing to some. We can do the same kind of harm. By using medical skills doctors can impose healing on people who do not want to be well. Sickness can be an escape from life or a way to handle life, a way to justify ourselves or to manipulate others.

The Role of a Christian Healer

Even Jesus did not force people to become well, and I do not think this should be the role of the doctor or the spiritual healer. Rather, the role of the Christian is to build a relationship with sick people, whether they come willingly or reluctantly for treatment. The Christian doctor ought to be uniquely aware of the inviolate right of the human soul and will for self-determination. He ought to be able to love in such a way that patients can respond to him and to God by saying, "Yes, I do want to be well." Then the doctor is free to use all the skills at his disposal to bring healing.

To me, our discussion at that luncheon meeting embodies some of the exciting new aspects of the transphysical dimension of life. Even doctors are discovering that there is something more important than health.

The Nature of Man

An increasing number of medical men today agree that man is made up of three parts—physical, mental, and spiritual. For this group of doctors, he is three in one and one in three, and any approach that does not take this into account will be inadequate and incomplete. In other words, the doctor is not dealing with a body, but with a person. The psychiatrist is not dealing with a mind and emotions but with a person. The clergyman is not ministering to a soul but to a person. When a person gets sick, more than his physical being has broken down, and a wise doctor has to treat more than physical symptoms and organs if he is to be adequate in the field of healing.

For a long time doctors who specialized in psychosomatic medicine, pioneers like Dr. Franz Alexander and Flanders Dunbar, advanced the theory that there are classic personality types associated with some major illnesses. Most clearly defined are the asthma type, the ulcer type, the migraine type, the rheumatoid arthritis type, and the cancer type. These pioneers insisted that emotional factors precipitated, or at least were associated with, many diseases. Later, other doctors turned this theory around and claimed that physical ailments were the cause of emotional disturbances or produced personality types.

Today both of these theories are up for grabs, and doctors speak with much less certainty. They are generally agreed, however, that ample research has shown a definite relationship of mind, body, and spirit. Doctors know that they have only uncovered the tip of an iceberg.

In researching for an article on this subject, *New York Times* science writer Jane E. Brody found widespread agreement in the medical profession that emotional changes in a person's life can precipitate physical changes. To put it in simple terms, your mind or your emotions can make your body sick, and in a tremendous variety of ways. The centuries-old belief that one can die of a broken heart or a crushed spirit has been borne out in many careful scientific studies.

The Body as a Spiritual Barometer

Our bodies are accurate spiritual barometers of what is happening to us inside in our thoughts and feelings. I used to suffer chronic colds, and through the first twenty years of my life, I could look forward to about a dozen of these a year. Since I've been a Christian, the number of colds has been considerably reduced. The thing I have observed is that, almost without exception, a cold follows a time of overwork and self-pity. It seems as though my body is saying, "Hear my needs. Care for me. Help me." Now I am sure that cold germs are always about in our society, but I am also convinced that changes in temperature, getting chilled or overheated, are often not the real causes of a cold. When I begin to need rest or just a little T.L.C., the germs are able to come in and do their work.

If this is true, then when my Christian friends see cold signs, they ought to be able to ask, "What is your body trying to say? What's your inner problem?"

Studies tell us that chronic tiredness is in the same category.

Exhaustion almost never comes from overwork. It comes, rather, from boredom or from the strain of trying to play a role. So, when people have some kind of physical collapse, the Christian community needs to help discern what the spiritual or emotional causes are and how they can be of help.

A personnel director for a large firm in New York City told me about his method of hiring people. He evaluates them not by their verbal answers to questions in interviews but by observing what their bodies say about them as they sit in the chair. For him the battery of questions he runs through is simply a smoke screen. This friend says that he gets much better results from simply reading the applicant's unconscious body reactions during the interview.

The behavioral sciences today are studying body language and have produced a number of intriguing books. One is William Schutz's *Here Comes Everybody* which examines body language at great length. Schutz himself, for example, has personally suffered from a sore left hip most of his life. He has finally associated this hip trouble with his inability to initiate things in life. His theory is that the left side of the body is the initiator. In marching we step out with the left foot. Boxers lead with their left hand. So Mr. Schutz sees the soreness of his left side as an unconscious unwillingness to take the initiative in social or interpersonal situations. As he has faced this and dealt with it, his sore left hip is becoming strong and healthy.

Some of our favorite expressions are also telltale signs of our inner feelings and thoughts. The words we use to show our frustration are revealing. A friend who used to work with me had suffered chronic migraines for years. When she was angry, her most frequent expression was "I wanted to blow my top." Well, migraines are literally blowing one's top! We hear other people say, "What a pain in the neck!" or "Oh, my aching back!" Chance phrases like these are often related to actual trouble spots in the body.

Reconciling the Physical and Spiritual

Jesus Christ came to reconcile each of us to God, to one another, to the world, and to ourselves. Part of being reconciled to ourselves is to be reconciled to our bodies. Your body is your friend, not your enemy. When your body breaks down, it is not failing you. On the contrary, it is struggling with conflicts and decisions and carrying burdens that you have not yet been able to handle consciously. And this is why an understanding of body language is so important. It can lead us to deeper truth about ourselves and other people.

In business, for example, when management avoids dealing with particular problems, they are pushed down to a level where the staff is forced to deal with them, usually in a more costly and inefficient way. When the administration and faculty of a school won't deal with controversial issues, the student body begins to deal with them, and we have all lived with the repercussions from this truth in recent years. In a church where the pastor and the official board do not deal with problems, the congregation has to live with them. In a society, when responsible government does not deal with problems, they move down to the grass roots and are the cause of riots and unrest. In families, when a husband and wife cannot deal with problems adequately, the children in the family have to live with and try to handle these unresolved tensions.

This is also true in the physical dimension. If you cannot deal with resentments, unhealed relationships, hidden sins, these are repressed until your body must deal with them. This is the whole premise of psychosomatic medicine. Your body becomes one who suffers for your inner self so that you can continue to exist in spite of tremendous unresolved problems.

I spoke about this on the West Coast recently, and at the close of the lecture someone came up with this response, "I suddenly realize that my body is a Christ-type. It is literally suffering and dying to give me more time to respond maturely to certain life situations. I am beginning to genuinely love my body and to be grateful for all it is bearing that my mind and spirit cannot face."

If our body is our best friend and suffering for us, we in the church need to take each other's physical problems seriously. It seems unfortunate that people with alcohol problems have had to go outside their own church to Alcoholics Anonymous. Overweight people have to find help from Weight Watchers. I thank God for these groups that are helping people to deal with their physical problems. But if the body is our friend, a part of our spirit and mind, then the church must have a ministry to the body, too. We might help each other answer questions like, "Why do I have that cold?" or "Why am I tired all the time?" or "Why am I overweight?" "Can you help me?" And we can begin a ministry to the body as part of our total ministry.

We need to understand that not only can the spirit make the body sick, but the body can also affect the spirit. Psychosomatic medicine is based upon a profound truth—the body and the spirit are a unity. As we begin to work with the body, make it a friend, listen to it, make it stronger and healthier, we will have a new doorway to the soul.

Sickness Comes in Spite of Understanding the Body— and Then Death

But a ministry to the body is not enough. Rollo May has said, that it is very unhealthy to worship mere health, and we must not produce adjustment at the expense of sensitivity and other things we ought to value more. No matter how skillful we may be at understanding our bodies and helping others understand theirs— there is the inevitable time for all of us when this earthly body breaks down.

I recently heard a speaker say among other things, "Make no mistake about it. God means to kill us all." Nevertheless, somehow most of us tend to feel that our own death is either impossible or so far in the future that it is irrelevant to current living. This speaker was reminding us that we have no choice at all about our eventual death, but we can choose our attitude towards death and, in some measure, the circumstances of our death. And, of course, we have much more choice as to how we live the days, weeks, months, or years between now and the time of our death. This is our temporal future.

Choosing Your Ground from Now Till Death

We cannot separate our present from our future. In one sense you are right now the person you're aiming at becoming. If you've ever driven a motorcycle you can appreciate this principle. You do not steer a motorcycle going forty miles an hour. You aim it. (This is probably true as well for a racing sailboat or a plane.) When I'm driving down the road I must look ahead for turns, curves, and other vehicles, and aim for openings.

Well, life is like that. We fix our eye on something we feel to be our destiny and then aim at it. From that moment on we are getting closer to our chosen destiny. For Christians this means asking God to show us what we're meant to be or do and then aiming at that.

A friend of mine in middle years, when most of her contemporaries were settling for the status quo, began to dream about her own destiny. Betty lives in Bermuda and had a concern for young people there with reading disabilities. There was no place on the island offering help or correction for that special problem. Having raised her own three children, Betty went off to Columbia University in New York, and got her master's degree in the area of psychology that deals with corrective reading. She has now set up a clinic in her Bermuda home that has already been a blessing to countless young people. Their lives are different because Betty dared to claim her destiny and aim her whole life at an opening she saw.

In a profound sense, we all become what we aim at. You are your dreams. T. E. Lawrence says, "All men dream . . . but not equally. They who dream by night in the dusty recesses of their minds wake in the day to find that it is vanity; but the dreamers of the day are dangerous men for they act out their dream with open eyes, to make it possible."

I could not agree more. The Bible is full of this kind of daytime dreaming. John writes in Revelation, "I saw a new heaven and a new earth" (Rev. 21:1). These daytime dreamers of God's have the power to bring their dreams into reality to change and shape things for others.

Freud had a great deal to say about the power of a mother or a father's dream in shaping the destiny of a child. I dare say that many of you reading this are, today, something of a projection of the dream your parents had for you. And if you have children your dreams are beginning to shape them. I don't know if we can eliminate or change this factor, or if we would want to. Sometimes our dreams for our children or our parents' dreams for us have been a detriment, but the point is that our dreams about the future for someone else can become a powerful shaping force.

Our futures are inextricably bound up with our present. Many of us are stuck in the present because our dreams for our own future are not large enough or because they need to be cut down to something that is manageable and life-size. Many of us in the latter situation have our lives and future dreams so complex and cluttered with things we ought to do that there is no clarity, no cutting edge.

To me this underscores a need for a simplified sense of destiny. And the Christian adventure with fellow dreamers and doers has been a great help in sorting things out. The alternative for me is a confusion so crippling it crushes life in the present.

Death is a reality. Not to reckon with that is foolish. Let's start today in the present to claim the future that God has for each one of us.

MEMORANDUM

TO: Keith

FROM: Bruce

RE: Chapter Twelve—Sickness and Death

Dear Keith:

This is another hard one. And I see that I barely mentioned death. (Does that mean anything, Sigmund?)

How about going into the deeper issues **underlying** specific illness and death and talking a little about the question of good and evil? Why do we Christians have to go through suffering after we are committed to Christ? How can we try to grasp the meaning of sickness? What are some of the world's notions about death? And does Jesus Christ offer us anything to do about it now? Finally how does being with him on his adventure give us hope or prepare us for death?

Bruce

P.S. Sorry this is the last memo. It's been fun (Phil. 1:6)!

"WHY? Why did our child have to be born a mongoloid?"

"Why did my wife get cancer at thirty-five with four young children to raise?"

"Why was my father killed in a head-on collision by a drunk swinger?"

These questions from the drawn haunted faces of grieving, frustrated Christians keep coming back to me in the quiet of my study. Why indeed?

I have faced questions like these in my own life before and after trying to make a serious commitment of my life to Christ. I have cried, prayed, read, asked, and thought about the meaning of sickness and death. When I was eighteen years old, I walked through the grief of a war telegram announcing the death of my only brother in a plane crash and absorbed what this did to my parents' lives. I saw my mother have a nervous breakdown and then sat by her as she died of cancer in a few years. My father had ulcers and then a heart condition which combined to kill him when I was twenty-three. And in the midst of these sicknesses I broke my neck in a car wreck, and the doctor thought I might be paralyzed.

When each member of my family died, I planned funerals and tried to console the ones who remained. As each one "disappeared," I spent a lot of time as a young man thinking about sickness and death. I watched how they affected us all—the bad effects and the *good*. And I can remember looking up at the stars late the night we heard of my brother's death, and crying out in my loneliness and frustration, "Why?"

The Question of Good and Evil

Since I have become a Christian I have seen that this scream is a way of asking probably the deepest and most perplexing question which faces a person who believes in the God of Jesus Christ: "If God is all-powerful and also good, why does he allow evil and pain to plague his people?"

As I was thinking back just now, I realized that this was one of the first questions which my mind went to after my conversion. About that time I remember backing out of our driveway one day. I had noticed absent-mindedly that our small daughter, who was then about four, was playing in the yard with her dolly near the driveway. But my mind was already at the office as I started the engine. Looking in the rear view mirror, I put the car in reverse and backed out of the garage. Suddenly I heard a sort of snapping "crunch" and then a scream. My stomach knotted and my throat tightened. As I jumped out of the car, all I could think about was, "O dear God, I've killed her!"

But I had not. She was standing beside the car with her shattered dolly in her arms sobbing her heart out. And through her tears came rage, hurt, and frustration in the accusation, "You've killed my baby!" She would not be consoled by promises of another doll or by anything I could say.

Irreparable Loss—a Difficult School

As I thought about that scene, I realized that this was her first conscious encounter with irreparable loss. As painful as it was, it gave her some of the experience she would need as an adult to deal with life, relationships, sickness, and death. Without such experiences to teach her about grief and life, her first exposure might be the death of her own child. And she might well lose her balance if she had no experience of expressing her honest rage and pain.

But I realized that she couldn't even imagine any possible benefit now. All she could grasp was the tragedy in her arms in that moment, and it was real. Maybe, I thought, from God's eternal perspective we adults are like four-year-old children, getting to know and feel the fabric of good and evil in life. Perhaps we are in a larger process of maturing than we can see from our limited and materialist immersion in our tiny worlds. And if God is in the business of creating a family of sons and daughters who are to have the kind of sensitive wisdom and loving-kindness which can *enter men's suffering with them,* perhaps firsthand experience of evil, of sickness and death, are in some way necessary for all of us Christians.

But having been through some of these things, I saw how pale and unsatisfactory such an analogy can be while the acid in one's stomach is churning. And I realized that in sickness and death we are facing a grim riddle which cannot be "solved" by a neat formula or analogy.

Some Basic Ideas about Sickness

Out of their uncertainty, Christians have come up with three basic notions about sickness—with dozens of variations. Some say, "Sickness is God's will, therefore we must bear it patiently." Others say, "Sickness is of Satan. And if we pray and have faith, God will root it out and heal us." Still others believe that "out of sickness can come understanding, noble character and achievements which would never otherwise have been." But having studied the Scriptures and having read many books on sickness and the whole problem of undeserved evil, I have not found any theoretical solution which satisfies the pain of the human soul in its agony and tells us "why."

From the Head to the Heart—Incarnational Understanding

How then do we Christians face sickness when it strikes us, or the people we love, on the adventure?

In a generation of mathematical and statistical abstractions we seem to have forgotten some of the very earthy truths about life which transcend the flimsy syllogisms of human thought. Modern psychology is rediscovering that there are aspects of human truth which are almost visceral—so tied to the body and the common experience of its life that they cannot be known apart from it.

As J. S. Whale explains it, "The problem of Evil is like the riddle of the Sphinx. The Sphinx was a terrible monster with the head of a woman and the body of a lion, which stationed itself beside the highway outside the ancient city of Thebes. It propounded a riddle to all who passed by, and devoured them because they could not solve it: 'What is it that goes on four feet in the morning, on two at noon and on three in the evening?' Oedipus went out to face the monster and answered correctly: 'Man, in his infancy, his full growth, and when he totters on his staff in old age.' The Sphinx gave a hoarse cry, and as it fled away, Oedipus drove it over a precipice." The story seems to mean that a riddle to which the answer is a basic principle of life is insoluble by the intellect but can be triumphantly solved in terms of *common experience and life*. "The real issues of life can be solved only in terms of life's experience, and not of any intellectual theory. It is when the problem of evil is deliberately shifted from the purely intellectual to the practical plane—out of the philosophers' classrooms into the street, the hospital ward, the personal encounter, or the sanctuary—that it becomes its own answer." [1]

And in the Incarnational gospel, Jesus Christ gives us something which is more valuable than intellectual answers to the deepest problems of human life. With his usual offer of freedom for the captive, God gives us a choice of whether we want his gift of life *in our experience* which will allow us to transcend and even utilize the circumstances which have us blocked. But to incorporate Jesus' answers in our lives, we must move beyond the question of *"Why* illness?" to "What can I *learn* from my illness?" One person learns patience, understanding, and compassion for others; another becomes unbearable. The choice can be with us.

Is Sickness a Good Thing?

But if it can be valuable, then is sickness a *good* thing? The Gospels and the church give a resounding "No!"

Here we have another of the many paradoxes of life and faith. Although disease *can* bring great advances in the Godlike qualities of human character, it can also destroy all a person's values. Christian doctors are right, I think, in giving their lives to snatch people from it, as Jesus did. For it certainly seems obvious that Jesus rejected entirely the idea that sickness was sent by God as a punishment. As Louis Cassels [2] points out, Jesus did not encourage the belief that the sufferer ought to *remain* ill in order to acquire courage or learn patience. In fact the Gospels report nineteen specific instances, and allude to hundreds of others, in which Jesus healed sick people by word or gesture. Christ anticipated modern medical science by recognizing that all illness is to some degree psychosomatic—involving the mind as well as the body. And his conversations with the sick always show a concern for the mind and the spirit as well as the body. He did not give people rational closure or a theory of sickness. He gave them *a way through* the sickness to God and his sensitive love.

There was something more that he came to do than heal the body. And only as a Christian goes through a serious illness himself or sits beside a loved one who does, can he have even a chance to experience God's "answer" to sickness and pain. Often the positive value can only be seen in retrospect.

Do you know any old people who are sensitive and really adept at helping others through crises who have never been through any themselves? These older, caring people may appear to be untouched by life, because of the positive and even joyful quality of their lives. But scratch the surface of one of God's saints and you will find scars of pain which came from encounters in the past with sickness, death, rejection, disappointment, or other personal tragedy. Apparently the sort of wisdom and loving-kindness which express God's sort of love are given their deepest colors and textures only through experiencing some of the sweat and unhappiness which come through encounters with evil and death.

Death

I have really resisted writing this section. So many Christian writers gloss over the reality of death and slide quickly to the "glories of the Resurrection." And often the implication is that any Christian who is really afraid of death doesn't have the true faith. But I'm going to try not to do this, because there are times when I've waked up from a dream terrified that I was dying—and that's been *since* I've become a Christian.

After birth, death is the most real and universal fact of human existence. As Myron Madden has said, we do not have to take it on faith that we all will die—as we do the resurrection of the dead for instance.[3] And whatever else there may be, we know that death will end the only life and relationships we know in the form in which we now experience them.

In the fact that we human beings are the only animals aware of time in a way that allows us to *know* we are going to die lie both the curse and the creative potential of human life.

With the knowledge of our own death, depicted dramatically in the Adam and Eve story in Genesis, comes a knowledge that we only have a limited amount of time in which to do what we want to with our lives. And this awareness forces us to *choose* and makes us acutely conscious of the fact that we must work "while it is yet day." In this way death becomes the great motivator to creative action. And most of our major choices reveal our conscious or unconscious beliefs about the fact and meaning of death.

Repression of Death and Attempted Material Solutions

In order to cope and focus on the problems and joys of living, most people repress the fact of their own death. I remember that I was not consciously afraid to die until several years *after* I became a Christian. Before that time I simply thought I was brave. Then finally I had enough security in Christ that circumstances could force me into facing and coming to terms with my own death to the extent that I have. And I think this is an essential part of growing up.

But if a person represses his death from consciousness, as people seem to do most of the time, then he may begin gathering money, possessions, friends, power, and prestige, or even Bible verses in a frantic unconscious attempt to assure himself that he will be secure—if he can just get enough of these things in his emotional bank account. But Jesus said to the man who kept building bigger barns, "You fool, this very night you must surrender your life"! It seems to me that he was trying to tell us that no amount of wealth can give life or save it (see Luke 12:17–21). All of our attempts to outwork and outsmart death are in vain.

Humanistic Solutions

People who do not believe in God but believe in a "moral universe" sometimes become social workers, doctors, or teachers —unconsciously or consciously aligning themselves and their lives on the side of mercy, healing, and growth. They can then justify their existence and also aid the forces of life in trying to push back the tide of evil and death. And through trying to live a righteous life, they can do the finest thing they can see available to man— and if there is any reward for goodness, now or later, they will be in the running for it.

Others get a glimpse at the fact that, like the animals, they are going to die. And they frantically devote their lives to the animal sensuous pleasures "while they can," repressing and running from death till it overtakes them.

Still others become stoics and concentrate on looking death in the face with courage.

Into this world of different reactions to death, all reflected in the various life-styles of the Gentiles—and the Jews—of his day, came Jesus of Nazareth with "good news" from God.

Sickness and Death / 241

The Gospel of Life

Contrary to much Christian thinking, I see Jesus' teachings concentrating on a way of *living* more than a rescue operation from death. Of course, it is true that his message indicated that ultimate justice takes place beyond death (e.g., see the story of the rich man and Lazarus, Luke 16:19–31). But Jesus came bringing a way to begin living in God's Kingdom *in this present existence.* This way gives people a quality of experience here and now that allows them to *know* in their very bloodstream, as it were, that they have in some sense *already* transcended the limitations of life imposed by death. As one commits his life to Jesus Christ and sees the miracle of the removal of his own blindness and fear of living, he starts relating to God and his Christian brothers in a new way. One by one, the biblical promises that God's children can become salt, light, and yeast to the world begin to take place in the follower's experience in the Christian family. As one believes Jesus at ever deeper levels *because of his own experience,* then the promise that "in my father's house are many rooms" (John 14, RSV) can imperceptibly become a personal assurance —not of a gold-streeted heaven, but that God who can transform one's whole experience of *living* can also handle the problem of *death.*

But unwittingly we American Christians have made it almost impossible for some people raised in the church to connect Jesus with *life.* Some little children in the presence of the lifeless body of a dead mother or grandparent in a casket are told "It's all right, honey, she's gone to be with Jesus." But from the small child's perspective a very different message may come through. The child may get the impression that Jesus mysteriously "gathers people up" and takes them away from those they love, or maybe even causes their death—because he wants them to be with him. This fear is repressed. But later, when one is called to "give his life to Jesus," an enormous resistance may be encountered for no conscious reason, because Jesus was identified with the "grim reaper" in a child's mind.

We Give Death Its "Power"

Another thing we have done which keeps us from seeing the gospel as an eternal quality and style of *life* is that through folklore, poetic imagery, and our habit of painting the dead to look lifelike, we have acted as if death is or has a real power or energy in itself. But it does not![4]

Death is in itself only a point on a journey. And often by the time it arrives it is a welcome point of peace and release. But it has no energy to "get us" through disease, etc., except that which we attribute to it through our imagination. We imagine ghosts in cemeteries and are exhausted after walking through one at night. But there were no ghosts, and the energy we used up in fear was all generated by us as we gave to death a power it would never have if *we* did not furnish it.

So if we can learn to live the quality of life Christ came to bring us here and now, then our energies and imagination will be captured by God and the thrust of life of which he is the source. And if we commit the power of our lives to him, we will have already overcome the power of death. When this happens, death somehow loses its horror, its "sting," and we are able to see it as a part of our common journey. Then our hope in Christ can blend into a hope in the resurrection which is not a frantic repressive cover-up of the fact of death, but rather is a natural part of the adventure of living for God.

Whatever "beyond death" may include (if anything), I find I have a growing conviction that the relationship with God and with his family will somehow continue. The best and most creative source of reality I've found *in this life* is in trying to respond to Christ and to his people. So my faith is more in the continuing presence of God himself and his concern for me—rather than in any images of the specific nature of a heaven beyond life.*

When I think of my own death, I become a child again in my imagination standing before the huge doors of a great mystery. My studies in theology and psychology fade into insignificance. And my trust in God is of the primitive nature of a small boy believing his father. It is somehow as if he had taken me as a child on a fascinating adventure with some people I grew to love. He had taught me, accepted me as I was, and showed me some invaluable truths about life. And along the way he told me, "Someday I'm going to take you on a greater trip than you can imagine, to a place where you have never been." Of course, I

---

* My wife, Mary Allen, first shared this idea with me years ago. For some helpful passages in the Bible regarding death see Psalms 27, 39, 46, 90, 121, and 130; John 14:1–4; Romans 8:14–39; and 1 Corinthians 15.

Sickness and Death / 243

couldn't envision the trip without more details. But because of the great adventure we already shared, I could believe him and not be afraid. I would have no idea how he was going to manage to take me on this trip. But I'd have great confidence that my Father would be able to handle the details and would finally bring me *home with him* wherever the end of the journey—the end of the Adventure—might be.

Notes

Chapter 1
1. Friedrich von Hügel, *Selected Letters of Baron Friedrich von Hügel*, ed. Bernard Holland (New York: E. P. Dutton, 1927), p. 305.
2. Ibid.
3. Carlos Castaneda, *Tales of Power* (New York: Simon and Schuster, 1974).
4. Nikos Kazantzakis, *Zorba the Greek* (New York: Simon and Schuster, 1953).

Chapter 2
1. Paul Tournier, *To Resist or To Surrender?*, trans. John S. Gilmour (Atlanta: John Knox, 1964), p. 49.
2. Father Andrew, *The Life and Letters of Father Andrew*, ed. Kathleen E. Burne (London: A. R. Mowbray, 1961).
3. Oswald Chambers, *My Utmost for His Highest* (New York: Dodd, Mead & Co., 1963), p. 339.
4. Blaise Pascal, *Pensées* (New York: E. P. Dutton, 1958), p. 97.

Chapter 3
1. Katherine Anne Porter, *Ship of Fools* (Boston: Little, Brown & Co., 1962).
2. *Washington Post*, 9 October 1972.
3. Reuel Howe, *The Miracle of Dialogue* (New York: Seabury, 1963), p. 84.
4. Henri Nouwen, *The Wounded Healer: Ministry in Contemporary Society* (New York: Doubleday, 1972), pp. 72–73.

Chapter 4
1. Dag Hammarskjöld, *Markings* (New York: Alfred A. Knopf, 1966), p. 63.
2. Martin Luther, *Luther's Works* (Philadelphia: Fortress Press, 1959), 36:86.
3. John Calvin, *Institutes of the Christian Religion*, Book III, Chapt. IV, para. 12.
4. Albert Camus, *The Fall*, quoted in Robert A. Raines, ed., *Creative Brooding* (New York: Macmillan, 1966), p. 106.

5. William James, *Varieties of Religious Experience* (New York: Random House, Modern Library, 1929), pp. 452–53.
6. Paul Tournier, *Guilt and Grace* (New York: Harper & Row, 1962), p. 114.

Chapter 5
1. Reinhold Niebuhr, *The Nature and Destiny of Man* (New York: Scribner's, 1941), 1:94. See also D. M. Baillie, *God Was In Christ* (New York: Scribner's, 1948), pp. 162 f., for Baillie's view on modern man's lack of a sense of sin.

Chapter 6
1. Karl Bucher, *Industrial Evolution* (New York: Henry Holt, 1901), p. 57.
2. Peter Kropotkin, *Mutual Aid* (New York: McLure, Phillip & Co., 1902), p. 90.
3. Will Durant, *Story of Civilization,* vol. 1, *Our Oriental Heritage* (New York: Simon & Schuster, 1935), p. 18.
4. Carl Jung, quoted in Calvin S. Hall and Gardner Lindzey, *Theories of Personality* (New York: John Wiley & Sons, 1957), p. 91.
5. Jolande Jacobi, *The Psychology of Carl Jung* (New Haven: Yale University Press, 1962), p. 144.

Chapter 7
1. Paul Tournier, *The Strong and the Weak* (Philadelphia: Westminster, 1963).
2. William Schutz, *Here Comes Everybody: Body, Mind and Encounter Culture* (New York: Harper & Row, 1971).

Chapter 8
1. William H. Masters and Virginia E. Johnson, *Human Sexual Response* (Boston: Little, Brown, 1966); *Human Sexual Inadequacy* (Boston: Little, Brown, 1970); *The Pleasure Bond* (Boston: Little Brown, 1975).
2. Charlie Shedd, *The Stork Is Dead* (Waco, Texas: Word Books, 1968), pp. 70–73.
3. Thomas à Kempis, *The Imitation of Christ* (London: William Collins, 1957), p. 50.

Chapter 10
1. I am indebted to Dr. Findley Edge for some of the criteria and ideas in this discussion, learned from him in a private conversation in 1964.
2. Jacobi, *The Psychology of Carl Jung,* p. 124. For an excellent biblical basis for a similar conclusion about the Christian life see

John Knox's book on Romans, *Life in Christ Jesus* (New York: Seabury, 1966), chapters 5–8.
3. William Temple, *Nature, Man and God* (New York: Macmillan, 1956), p. 239.
4. Paul Tournier, *The Adventure of Living* (New York: Harper & Row, 1965), pp. 149–50.

Chapter 11
1. Paul Tournier, *A Place For You* (New York: Harper & Row, 1968).
2. Ibid.
3. C. S. Lewis, Mere Christianity (New York: Macmillan, 1960).

Chapter 12
1. J. S. Whale, *The Christian Answer to the Problem of Evil,* 2nd ed. (London: SCM Press, 1939), pp. 36–37.
2. Louis Cassels, *The Real Jesus* (New York: Doubleday, 1968), p. 26.
3. Much of the discussion in this section comes after reading Myron Madden's perceptive book *Raise the Dead!* (Waco, Texas: Word Books, 1975), which I heartily recommend for a clarification, expansion and correction of some of these points.
4. Madden, *Raise the Dead!*. See, for instance, pp. 22, 28.

Sources

We express appreciation to the following publishers for permission to reprint and, where necessary, adapt copyrighted material in this book:

ZONDERVAN PUBLISHING HOUSE for material from Bruce Larson, *Dare to Live Now* © 1965; Bruce Larson, *Living on the Growing Edge* © 1968; Bruce Larson, *Setting Men Free* © 1967. Used by permission.

WORD BOOKS for material from Bruce Larson, *No Longer Strangers* © 1971; Bruce Larson, *Ask Me to Dance* © 1972; Bruce Larson, *The One and Only You* © 1974; Keith Miller, *The Taste of New Wine* © 1965; Keith Miller, *A Second Touch* © 1967; Keith Miller, *Habitation of Dragons* © 1970; Keith Miller, *The Becomers* © 1973. Used by permission.

Faith at Work for material from the following issues: April, October, 1971; August, October, 1972; June, October, 1973; February, April, June, August, October, 1974; February, March, August, 1975.

	Pages in this book	*Pages in original source*
Chapter 1	14–15	Miller, *Habitation of Dragons,* 166–67
	19–20	Miller, *Habitation of Dragons,* 183–84
	22–24	Larson, *Faith at Work,* October 1974
	24–26	Larson, *Faith at Work,* March 1975
Chapter 2	37–40	Larson, *No Longer Strangers,* 63–64, 70–71, 79–90 *passim*

Sources

	Pages in this book	Pages in original source
	40–41	Larson, *Faith at Work,* April 1971, August 1972
	41–43	Larson, *Living on the Growing Edge,* 19–20, 17, 24–25
Chapter 3	47–50	Larson, *Setting Men Free,* 27–30, 32–34
	50–53	Larson, *The One and Only You,* 131–32, 136–40
Chapter 4	65–73	Larson, *Ask Me to Dance,* 43–50, 51–53
	73–74	Larson, *Dare to Live Now,* 51–52
Chapter 5	87–88	Larson, *Faith at Work,* February 1974
	88–92	Larson, *Faith at Work,* August 1974
	92–96	Larson, *Faith at Work,* June 1973*
	98–109	Miller, *The Taste of New Wine,* 89–101
Chapter 6	114–119	Larson, *Faith at Work,* August 1975
	124–126	Miller, *Faith at Work,* August 1975
Chapter 7	131, 132–134	Larson, *Faith at Work,* February 1975
Chapter 8	147–56	Larson, *Ask Me to Dance,* 91–101
	162–66	Miller, *A Second Touch,* 97–105
Chapter 9	169–75	Larson, *The One and Only You,* 51–55, 38–39, 44–46, 109–10
	177–80	Miller, *The Taste of New Wine,* 69–73
	181–83	Miller, *A Second Touch,* 51–54
	183–84	Miller, *The Becomers,* 136
Chapter 10	187–88	Larson, *Faith at Work,* June 1974

Sources / 251

Pages in this book	Pages in original source
188–89	Larson, *Ask Me to Dance,* 18–20
189–94	Larson, *Faith at Work,* April 1974
197–202, 203	Miller, *The Becomers,* 141–49, 158

Chapter 11

207–214	Miller, *The Becomers,* 159–70, 173–76
216–219	Larson, *The One and Only You,* 15–22 *passim*
219–222	Larson, *Faith at Work,* October 1972
222	Larson, *The One and Only You,* 100

Chapter 12

225–28	Larson, *Faith at Work,* October 1971
228–31	Larson, *Ask Me to Dance,* 86–89
231–33	Larson, *Faith at Work,* October 1973

* This article adapts material from Larson, *The One and Only You,* pp. 125–27, 132–33.

(continued from back cover)

Christ, we are in the process of changing and becoming whole people, reaching out with open and creative hands toward life, people, work, and God.

Keith Miller and Bruce Larson are both professional writers and lecturers, but each speaks from his own perspective. Keith is a layman who was in the oil exploration business for many years. Bruce is an ordained minister. Both are students of psychology and theology.

The twelve "hidden difficulties" discussed by Keith and Bruce in **Living the Adventure** are also part of a thirteen-week study course of the same name. The course includes study guides, a leader's guide, and three cassette tapes.

Living the Adventure takes up where the authors' first group study, **The Edge of Adventure,** left off. In that book and course, Bruce and Keith asked what would happen if we tried to live our whole lives for a certain period as if we believed totally in God. The twelve studies dealt with such things as life before a Christian commitment, taking the gamble of commitment, prayer, the Bible, the church, family and job relationships. **The Edge of Adventure** provided an itinerary of "first steps" for those just starting out on the Christian life.

For those who are now on their way, **Living the Adventure** will provide the challenge and encouragement to continue growing as Christians.

WORD BOOKS, Publisher   98055
Waco, Texas

Jacket design: Dennis Hill